Gerald R. Ford

38th President of the United States

Known and respected for hard work and team spirit, Gerald Ford assumed the role of 38th President of the United States during a turbulent period in American history. He was the first man to become chief executive of the nation without being elected to either the presidency or the vice-presidency. (Gerald R. Ford Library.)

Gerald R. Ford
38th President of the United States

David R. Collins

 GARRETT EDUCATIONAL CORPORATION

Manufactured in the United States of America

Edited and produced by Synthegraphics Corporation

Library of Congress Cataloging in Publication Data
Collins, David R.   *323835-2*
  Gerald R. Ford, 38th President of the United States / David R. Collins.
    p.   cm. — (Presidents of the United States)
  Includes bibliographical references.
  Summary: Presents the life of Gerald Ford, including his childhood, education, employment, and political career.
  1. Ford, Gerald R., 1913- . —Juvenile literature.
2. Presidents—United States—Biography—Juvenile literature.   3. United States—Politics and government—1974-1977—Juvenile literature.   [1. Ford, Gerald R., 1913- .
2. Presidents.]   I. Title.   II. Series.
E866.C65   1990
973.925'092—dc20
[B]
[92]   89-39945
ISBN 0-944483-65-8   CIP
                                                  AC

Contents

Chronology for Gerald R. Ford

1913	Born on July 14 in Omaha, Nebraska
1915	Moved to Grand Rapids, Michigan
1917	Adopted by Gerald Rudolf Ford
1931	Graduated from South High School
1935	Graduated from University of Michigan
1935–1940	Boxing coach and assistant varsity football coach at Yale University
1938–1941	Attended Yale University Law School
1941–1942	Practiced law in Grand Rapids
1942–1946	Enlisted as an ensign in U.S. Navy and served in various assignments
1946–1949	Practiced law in Grand Rapids
1948	Married Betty Warren on October 15
1949–1973	Served in the U.S. House of Representatives
1973	Confirmed as Vice-President on December 6
1974–1977	Served as President of the United States
1976	Nominated as Republican candidate for President; defeated by Jimmy Carter
1979	Published autobiography *A Time to Heal*
1981	Dedicated Gerald R. Ford Library in Ann Arbor, Michigan, on April 27

Chapter 1

A Nation in Turmoil

he driver's hands tightened around the steering wheel as the car joined the stream of vehicles traveling the main thoroughfares of the nation's capital. The news on the car radio the morning of June 18, 1972, was most disturbing.

> . . . and the five men arrested inside of the Democratic headquarters at the Watergate complex last night were said to be in possession of electronic surveillance devices and cameras, apparently intended for some kind of 'bugging' operation . . .

Who could be so dumb? That's what Gerald Ford wondered as he threaded his car through the traffic. What was there to gain? If the intruders were Republicans, and that seemed most likely, Ford prayed that they were acting out of some misdirected sense of party loyalty and were not affiliated with any official Republican agency.

PRESIDENTIAL PROBLEMS

As House Minority Leader, Ford hardly needed any additional troubles. It was difficult enough to muster support behind the programs and policies of President Richard Nixon. Occasionally, the Republican chief executive won a positive following in Congress and the country, but such backing seldom lasted for long. Most recently, criticism of Nixon's actions in the handling of Vietnam and domestic problems had increased. Any association with an illegal break-in at the Democratic headquarters could cause serious damage to the Republicans.

The House Minority Leader tried to dismiss the matter from his mind. Certainly, there were more pressing concerns at hand, such as legislative duties that demanded his personal attention and the political savvy that he had accumulated from many years in government service. With a strong Republican sweep at the ballot box in November, Gerald Ford knew that he stood an excellent chance of becoming the Speaker of the House of Representatives. It was a longtime goal. But as Ford swung his car into his reserved parking place at the Capitol, he pushed such thoughts to the back of his mind. He stepped out of the car, ready to tackle the day-to-day matters that accompanied his role as House Minority Leader.

The Committee to Re-Elect the President

But when Ford learned later that one of the five men arrested was James McCord, the Republican leader was flabbergasted. McCord, a former employee of the Central Intelligence Agency (CIA), was presently working for the Committee to Re-Elect the President (CRP or "CREEP" as it was sometimes called). Ford, himself, was a member of the committee. Surely the committee chairman, John Mitchell, would never have authorized such a break-in. Why, Mitchell was a former United States Attorney General. As eager as he was to see Richard Nixon win another election, he would never sanction a break-in or burglary . . . or would he?

Then when Ford heard through the political grapevine that G. Gordon Liddy might have something to do with the events at Watergate, the House Minority Leader grew even more concerned. Liddy was active in New York state Republican circles, but he was never known as a cooperative party player. "A maverick" some labeled him. Others called him "strange" or "off center." Liddy, too, was a member of the Committee to Re-Elect the President.

Ford took his concerns directly to John Mitchell. "Did you or anyone in the White House have anything to do with the Watergate break-in?" asked the House Minority Leader. "Absolutely not," Mitchell replied. "What about the President?" Ford continued. He was convinced that he already knew what the answer would be, but he wanted to be sure.

John Mitchell's gaze was steadfast, his eyes looking straight into Ford's. "Absolutely not," was the answer one more time.

The Election of 1972

Again, Gerald Ford put the Watergate matter aside. As a Republican and the House Minority Leader, there was much to do before the fall election campaign. On his visit to China in February, President Nixon had opened the doors for people to travel between that country and the United States. Ford and Democratic Leader Hale Boggs, their families, and staffs were scheduled for a summer visit to China. Then it would be back to America for a crowded calendar of campaigning.

When the Democrats' nominated George McGovern to oppose Nixon in November, Ford was delighted. Because there was dissension among Democrats concerning the selection of McGovern as the party candidate, the stage was set for a Republican landslide. Even though the Watergate affair continued to make the news, with one name leading to another, the entire incident was never totally resolved. But President Nixon's declarations that "such actions have no place in the American electoral process" and "the White House had no involvement" satisfied most people. It was certainly good enough for Gerald Ford.

Thus, in November, Richard Nixon won by a large margin, while voters in his Michigan district sent Gerald Ford back to the House of Representatives. However, the Republicans captured no majority in either the Senate or the House. Gone was Ford's dream of becoming House Speaker, a position that went to the majority party in the House. By early 1973, Ford had decided to run for Congress just one more time, then retire in January of 1977. Leaving office as the leader of his party in the House was no small accomplishment.

CAMPAIGN SABOTAGE

At the same time that Gerald Ford was evaluating his own political future, events were unfurling that would cast an ominous shadow over the country. It was clear that the break-in at the Democratic headquarters at Watergate was not an isolated attempt by five men acting on their own. Far from it. Two reporters from the *Washington Post*, Bob Woodward and Carl Bernstein, had already pieced together parts of an intricate scheme leading into the offices of high government officials.

The United States Senate was probing the matter, too. Accusations of secret and illegal campaign sabotage filled the air and the media. Despite repeated denials by Republican officials of any wrongdoing, including President Nixon, evidence continued to mount of White House involvement.

Unwavering Trust

Although Gerald Ford had served in Congress for 25 years, there were many of his colleagues who considered him naive, almost too trusting. As more and more of the Watergate evidence pointed to the involvement of top-level Republican office-holders and appointees, Ford maintained an adamant position of disbelief. "What! Do you think the President of the United States would lie?" Ford declared, in answer to one reporter's question. "Just the thought of an American President intentionally deceiving the people of this nation repulses me."

At a Republican gathering back home in Michigan, Ford declared that all administration personnel being accused of taking part in Watergate should go before the Senate committee investigating the matter and deny any involvement in the affair. "Surely a public denial under oath would squelch many of these evil rumors," he insisted.

Ford's trust in President Nixon did not waver. Publicly, the House Minority Leader bravely upheld his party's chieftain and the nation's elected leader. He rallied support for the President's policies and programs in Congress, personally voting for Nixon's proposals 83 percent of the time. But the nationally televised Watergate hearings during the summer of 1973 continued to impair the credibility of the President of the United States. For the first time, there were officials calling for the impeachment (removal from office for misconduct) or resignation of President Nixon.

A committee from the House of Representatives was appointed to investigate the charges against the President. Through all of this, the White House attempted to promote a "business as usual" atmosphere, constantly trying to play down the Watergate controversy. Ford's efforts to move legislative programs through the House were largely ignored as members of Congress attempted to deal with the ever-escalating Watergate quagmire. Daily headlines heralded new developments, ranging from the criminal trials of some of the participants to surprise revelations from witnesses testifying before committees probing the situation.

ANOTHER SCANDAL

With the nation already whirling in political turmoil, there was hardly need for another scandal. Yet that is just what happened, this time the shadow of greed and corruption falling upon the vice-presidency. The man occupying that position, Spiro Agnew, was accused of accepting bribes while serving as governor of Maryland. Professing his innocence, Agnew nonetheless resigned from office in order to avoid criminal prosecution. As of October 10, 1973, the United States had no Vice-President, and calls for President Nixon's resignation were increasing each day.

Under the circumstances, the need for a Vice-President was desperate. Spiro Agnew was only the second Vice-President in United States history to resign, the first being John C. Calhoun in 1832, who resigned to become a senator from South Carolina. Thankfully, only six years before, in 1967, the 25th Amendment to the Constitution had been passed; it provided for the replacement of the Vice-President. A majority of the members of both the House of Representatives and the Senate was needed to approve any candidate suggested by the President. But who would that candidate be?

Weighing the Decision

In the days following Agnew's resignation, Ford was summoned to many meetings, including one with President Nixon. Although the position of Vice-President was not specifically offered to him, it was clear what top Republicans wanted to know: If offered, would Gerald Ford accept the vice-presidential appointment?

As he weighed the decision, Ford pondered the pros and cons. He had always hoped for and worked toward the position of Speaker of the House. As Vice-President, he would preside over the Senate, voting only when there were ties, and carrying out ceremonial tasks. No longer would he be able to initiate legislative programs and create policies. His family, too, would be more exposed to the media, undergoing far greater scrutiny than ever before. Was it worth it?

On the other hand, Ford knew he had many friends in Congress. Perhaps he might be able to mend political fences, push through Nixon's best programs, and ultimately, help strengthen a nation suffering from turmoil and strife. Ford let the word go out—he would accept the vice-presidential appointment if it was offered.

THE NEW VICE-PRESIDENT

The offer was not long in coming. On Saturday, October 13, President Nixon submitted to Congress the name of Gerald Ford to replace Spiro Agnew as Vice-President. In truth, Ford was not Nixon's first choice. That had been John Connally. But because the former governor of Texas lacked friends on Capitol Hill, he stood little chance of winning confirmation.

Two other top choices were Nelson Rockefeller and Ronald Reagan, but they might split the Republican Party between conservatives and moderates. It was too big a risk, especially at a time when Republican strength in the country was ebbing daily. Ford could win confirmation easily in Congress and satisfied most of the party hierarchy. At least, that was the Republican consensus.

Appointment Confirmed

Ford's confirmation hearing by the Senate and House went relatively smoothly, but not without some controversy. Twenty-five years in Washington had not been wasted; he proved an able and eloquent subject under examination. As to his personal political philosophy, Ford was ready with an answer that reflected his entire career: "Moderate in domestic affairs, conservative in fiscal affairs, and dyed-in-the wool internationalist in foreign affairs." His voice was firm without being bold; his convictions were deep and sincere. There were no evasive answers; little hesitation was shown.

Only one incident marred the confirmation process. A lobbyist (a person who tries to influence public officials on certain legislation) named Richard Winter-Berger testified that Ford had received some campaign contributions and personal cash payments in exchange for the granting of political favors.

Winter-Berger also suggested that Ford suffered from both mental and physical stress in his political position.

Despite the accusations, there was little if any proof to back them up. On November 27, 1973, the Senate voted 92 to 3 to approve Ford's nomination. He had survived the most exhausting investigation into his past by FBI agents, and passed with flying colors. Some two weeks later, on December 6, the members of the House also voted. They confirmed his nomination by a vote of 387 to 35.

Less than an hour later, Gerald Ford stood before a joint session of Congress and was sworn in as Vice-President of the United States. With his wife Betty holding the Bible on which his right hand rested, Ford repeated the oath of office administered by Warren Burger, Chief Justice of the Supreme Court. Looking on nearby was a smiling Richard Nixon, who hosted a party at the White House after the ceremonies. It had been a long time since Republicans had reason to celebrate, and they enjoyed the mood of the moment. The new Vice-President felt relaxed and comfortable.

Still Backing the President

But cause for celebration was brief. Now, with a new Vice-President in office, the calls for Nixon's impeachment grew even louder and more widespread. Gerald Ford had indeed pondered the possibility of assuming leadership of the nation. This had been one of the focal points of interrogation by members of the House of Representatives during the confirmation hearing.

But much of that questioning and answering had been purely hypothetical. Ford was still convinced that Nixon was innocent of any criminal wrongdoing. The President, Ford felt, simply seemed incapable of appreciating the amount of trouble he was in. When he did, surely he could and would prove himself innocent of the charges being hurled against him.

Facing Reality

But by early spring of 1974, every day revealed new and damaging revelations regarding White House involvement in the Watergate break-in and attempts among top Republican officials to cover up the incident. Now Gerald Ford was brought face-to-face with a potential reality. There was every likelihood that Richard M. Nixon—either by resignation or impeachment—would not complete his elected term of office as President of the United States.

Following a press conference, one reporter's question continued to nag Ford. "Given the mess you find yourself in, Mister Vice-President," asked the interrogator, "do you ever wish you would have chosen a less strenuous field of endeavor, something other than politics?"

Gerald Ford rubbed his chin and smiled. "Well, my friend, 'mess' is your word, not mine. I prefer the word 'challenge.' I have always welcomed a challenge. If I didn't, I would never meet with any reporters."

A light touch was often a trademark of Gerald Ford. In the gloomiest of moments, he frequently could find an uplifting quip, a positive remark. This moment was no exception, and the reporters chuckled.

But that night, Gerald Ford's thoughts reflected more seriously on the question asked of him earlier that day. For so long, every minute had been spent considering the present and the future. Lately, when the past *was* recalled, it seemed that everything had begun on June 17, 1972, the night of the Watergate break-in. For Gerald Ford, however, everything had started long before that.

Chapter 2

Changes and Challenges

Omaha, Nebraska, is sometimes referred to as the city where either the West or the Midwest begins, depending on which way a traveler is heading. But there is no question about the origin of Gerald Ford—or, rather, Leslie Lynch King, Jr., for that was the original name of the 38th President of the United States. He was born in Omaha on July 14, 1913.

BACKGROUND OF PARENTS

Both Leslie Lynch King, Sr., and Dorothy Gardner were native midwesterners when they met and married in 1912. It was a quick courtship, perhaps too quick, for the marriage soon became a stormy one. The senior Lynch was a wool trader with a violent temper, often directed toward his wife. The quarrels were loud and frequent, and in 1915, a divorce was granted.

Dorothy then took her young son to Grand Rapids, Michigan, where her parents lived in a large house near Garfield Park. She soon attracted the attention of Gerald Rudolf Ford, a local paint salesman. On February 1, 1916, Dorothy and Gerald were married. After they moved into a two-family house on Madison Avenue, young Leslie Lynch

King, Jr., was legally adopted by his new stepfather in 1917. He officially became Gerald Rudolf Ford, Jr.

GROWING UP IN GRAND RAPIDS

The neighborhood kids around Madison Avenue delighted in the occasional fire alarms that came into Firehouse No. 7. It was the last fire station in the city to rely on horse-drawn equipment. To the accompaniment of clanging bells and screaming sirens, the firehouse doors would fling open, releasing teams of horses headed on their mission of mercy. It was a spectacular sight for youngsters, especially for a pre-school Jerry Ford.

A Fighting Student

At age five, Jerry began making the block and a half jaunt to Madison Elementary School. At this time, World War I was being fought in Europe "to make the world free for democracy." At Madison Elementary, Jerry Ford was doing his own fighting, often returning home from school with torn clothes, a dirty face, and skinned elbows and knees. The gravel playground behind school was the scene of his battles.

In the classroom, Jerry was an able student and made friends quickly. But when his temper flared, as it often did, he would get into a fight. Upon arriving home following an encounter, his mother would deal with the matter immediately. Imitating his angry face and heated remarks, she would apply a quick ear twisting and dispatch him to his room for quiet contemplation. Only after Jerry had calmed down was he allowed to discuss the cause of the confrontation. Active in many church and civic groups, as well as frequently baking bread and sewing clothes for family and friends, Dorothy Ford took her role as wife and mother very seriously.

Gerald Ford, Sr., was equally concerned with the well-

At age 11, young Jerry Ford was already assuming the reins of leadership, in this case, of a pioneer wagon train as part of a neighborhood parade in Grand Rapids, Michigan. (Gerald R. Ford Library.)

being of his family. He had worked his way up in the Grand Rapids Wood Finishing Company, and also shared an interest in the family coal business. Forced to leave school after the eighth grade due to his father's death and family responsibilities, he nonetheless recognized the importance of an education. Although active in the Masons, Elks, Boy Scouts (as an advisor), and church, he still placed a high priority on being a husband and father.

Quarantined

In July 1918, the Ford family welcomed a new addition—Tom. The infant came down with scarlet fever, which required the entire house to be quarantined. Young Gerald learned to hate the big sign on the front door that prohibited visitors and restricted his own activities. Only Dr. John Wright, the family doctor, was allowed to enter the house.

To everyone's relief, baby Tom finally pulled through, which allowed young Gerald to boast of his "superhuman" brother. Shortly afterwards, Jerry himself was hurried to the hospital for an emergency appendectomy. When it was found to be a false diagnosis, the entire family became more cautious about the world of medicine.

Family Responsibilities

In the early 1920s, the Ford family experienced some financial setbacks. When they lost the attractive home on Rosewood Avenue that they had acquired two years before, they moved to a smaller rented house on Union Avenue. While still in grade school, Jerry was banking the furnace before going to bed at night and removing the ashes at 6:00 A.M., before going to classes. Without complaint, he made his bed, helped clean the kitchen, and washed the dishes. As the family grew—Dick arrived in 1924 and Jim in 1928—household chores continued to be divided according to age.

Developing Character

During these years, Jerry's character began to be shaped by ideas and feelings that would last a lifetime. It was while in junior high school that he became especially sensitive to the competitive spirit that was developing among his friends and classmates. Rivalry sparked, whether the goal was the starting slot on a sports team, the lead in a play, or attention from "that certain girl." Because of their rivalry, several of Jerry's classmates found themselves hating each other, a waste of time in young Ford's opinion.

Jerry began to develop a philosophy that everyone had more good qualities than bad. By understanding one's positive traits and accentuating them, any individual was likely to get along much better with people. This attitude proved productive in making and keeping friends as Jerry passed through his school years. Later on, when he entered the political arena, that same philosophy would offer many rewards and pay rich dividends.

HIGH SCHOOL YEARS

By the time he reached South High School in Grand Rapids, Jerry was eager to test his athletic ability on the football field. He went out for the center position and, with the help of Coach Cliff Gittings, acquired the skill and discipline he needed to win a starting berth on the team as a sophomore. Quickness and accuracy were demanded, especially for the type of plays Coach Gittings emphasized. But the effort produced results, with the team winning the city championship and Jerry capturing a slot on the all-city top squad.

"Sports are fine," Jerry heard his parents say often, "but

A proud Gerald Ford, Sr., poses with his four sons—from left to right: Tom, Gerald, Jr., Dick, and baby Jim—in the late autumn of 1927. (Gerald R. Ford Library.)

you can't forget you're in school to earn the best grades you can." History and government proved to be Jerry's favorite subjects, with the young man never learning enough of the people and events that formed America. He did well in math, too, but science courses proved especially challenging. He struggled with chemistry and Latin and was delighted when he attained average marks in these courses.

His grades won Jerry recognition by the National Honor Society. Among the 220 members of his South High School class, he ranked in the top five percent. Jerry's achievements were even more impressive in light of the fact that he also juggled a variety of part-time jobs. These included mowing lawns, handling concessions at a local amusement park, and serving as cook, clerk, and dishwasher at a restaurant across the street from the high school.

Solving a Problem

But it was on the gridiron where Jerry Ford truly excelled. By the end of his junior year, he had not only won himself a secure position as center on the football team, he was tapped as captain-elect of the Trojans for his final year. During the summer of 1930, however, the Ford family moved to an old house in East Grand Rapids. Four miles away from South High, Jerry faced the gloomy prospects of having to attend another high school and not receiving his diploma among his friends and classmates of the past five years. He would also be giving up his leadership role on the football team.

Although sympathetic, his stepfather left it up to Jerry to work out the problem. In order to earn more money in addition to what he had already saved, Jerry took a job working at the Ford Paint and Varnish Company, which his stepfather had founded two years before. It was hard, smelly labor, cleaning paint vats and mixing and filling cans, but the pay was 40 cents an hour—a substantial amount for a high school student in those days. By the end of the summer, he bought his first car, a 1924 Ford coupe with a rumble seat. This would provide the means for him to get to and from South High School.

The car proved to be a worthwhile purchase indeed, for the Trojans went undefeated on the field, capturing the state high school football championship. Much of the credit went to the team's star center, Jerry Ford, who accepted the spotlight with poise and modesty.

A Trip to Washington

Capping off Jerry's senior year was an exciting trip to Washington, D.C., as part of a popularity contest. The Majestic, one of the biggest theaters in Grand Rapids, joined with movie houses in 50 other participating cities in the Midwest to select the "most popular senior" in the local high schools. People attending the Majestic wrote their choices on ballots and dropped them into a box in the lobby. Jerry could hardly believe the news when told that he had been picked.

After traveling to Chicago, where Jerry joined the other midwestern winners, the group went to the nation's capital for five days of sight-seeing. It was the beginning of the Great Depression, that period during the 1930s when millions of people were out of work, businesses and banks closed, and there was economic suffering across the nation. For the moment, however, Jerry cheerfully strolled through the halls of Congress and visited the White House.

The tall senior from Grand Rapids soaked in everything he saw, listening intently to guides and guards. As always, history was interesting, but Jerry Ford felt no great desire to seek any career in government. Certainly not as long as a career in sports was a possibility. He was just as eager to return to South High and the baseball diamond. Being left-handed made him a bit of a novelty at first base, where he displayed the same speed and precision that had earned him state honors on the gridiron.

FINDING A WAY

Jerry graduated from South High School in June of 1931. As far as college was concerned, money was a major obstacle. Like other businesses, the Ford Paint and Varnish Company was feeling the pangs of the Depression. Tom, Dick, and Jim Ford, Jerry's stepbrothers, were in various stages of their own education and funds were needed to get them through high school.

But there were others who recognized the promise and potential of the South High graduate. Certainly his football talents would make him a worthy catch, and the "B" average he had earned added to his luster. Michigan, Harvard, and Northwestern all extended invitations to him to visit their campuses and look over their sports and academic programs.

Picking the Wolverines

Jerry took advantage of the opportunities to visit the schools and was particularly impressed by Coach Harry Kipke and the University of Michigan at Ann Arbor. The Wolverine football team was greatly respected in the nation. Coach Kipke thought Jerry would be good for the team and promised to help him find work while he attended school. "You have bright prospects here at Ann Arbor," Kipke predicted.

Coach Gittings promised that the South High sports alumni would also try to help Jerry go to college. So did the school principal, Arthur Krause. There was a special bookstore scholarship of $100 available. That was enough for a full year's tuition. Although he did not know it at the time, Jerry's Uncles Roy and Ruah La Forge were also setting aside a fund that would provide him with two dollars of spending money each week while attending college.

At 18, Gerald Ford, Jr., was headed to the University of Michigan at Ann Arbor. He knew that many challenges lay before him. He hoped and prayed he could meet them successfully.

Chapter 3

Bright Prospects

Suitcase in hand, Jerry Ford surveyed the room before him. It was hardly a deluxe suite. Located on the third floor at the back of a rooming house, the room measured about ten-by-ten. For one person, it might be adequate enough. But the six-foot, 195-pound All-State center from Grand Rapids would be sharing the space with a roommate, a basketball player. With the two beds and the two desks, the floor space was virtually exhausted. One small window was to be shared.

The rent of four dollars a week would be split between the two roommates, keeping expenses to a minimum, and Coach Kipke had lined Jerry up with a job working at the university hospital in Ann Arbor. No, it might not be the most glamorous situation a person could find himself in, but in those Depression days, when people had no work and sometimes no home, Gerald Ford, Jr., considered himself pretty lucky. Quickly, the new Wolverine freshman tossed his suitcase on one of the beds and began to unpack.

LIFE AT ANN ARBOR

It was not long before Jerry discovered that his freshman English course would be a major struggle. Never a strong student in writing, he faced a new challenge each weekend as he labored over the 1,000-word theme that was due every Monday morning. The homework was sandwiched between football practice and waiting tables at the interns' dining room at the hospital. He also helped clean up the nurses' cafeteria.

Although Jerry was accustomed to plenty of playing time while a star center at South High, it was a totally different situation at the University of Michigan. Because the Wolverines already had an All-American center in Chuck Bernard, Jerry found himself spending a lot of time sitting on the bench. He would like to have been on the field himself, but with the Michigan squad posting win after win, he could hardly complain.

Money Problems

Money problems continued to haunt Jerry, despite his best efforts to budget carefully. Every three months, he visited the blood depository at the university hospital and collected $25 for giving a pint of blood. There were no more hours that he could work, no other ways to reduce expenses. Carefully Jerry tallied his bills for clothes, lodging, books, and supplies. He was shocked to discover the total was $600! This was far more than he had expected.

In desperation, Jerry wrote to his real father, who was now living in Wyoming. Perhaps he might be willing to help. But no answer came back. Again, Jerry pondered his problem. There was no more money available from home. His father was struggling just to keep the family business alive through the Depression.

Knowing that two friends of his parents, Mr. and Mrs. Ralph Conger in Grand Rapids, had recently come into an inheritance, Jerry wrote to them asking if they could help. It was not an easy letter to write, but Jerry promised to repay the loan as soon as possible. By return letter, he received a check for $600. It was clear that the Congers, like Coach Kipke, also believed that their young friend had "bright prospects."

A Dramatic Encounter

Although Jerry Ford had distinguished himself in football at Michigan from the first day he arrived on the field as a freshman, he was not able to rack up much actual playing time until his senior year. He eased smoothly into Chuck Bernard's position, hoping the 1934 team would pile up victories like those in past seasons. Injuries took their toll, however, weakening the Wolverine squad. Morale slowly ebbed away. But in the middle of a losing season, a dramatic encounter with Georgia Tech left an indelible mark on Jerry's mind and shifted Michigan into the winning column.

Willis Ward was a Wolverine standout, a young black man who had set college records in track. He was equally impressive on the gridiron. While the Wolverines were preparing themselves for the contest against the all-white Georgia Tech, news reached Ann Arbor that Georgia Tech refused to play unless Ward stayed on the bench. As a concession, the Georgia Tech coach agreed to bench one of his own star players.

Members of the Michigan team were shocked; Jerry felt the entire suggestion was morally wrong. Not only was Willis Ward a teammate, the two of them had roomed together often when the team traveled. Jerry called his stepfather to get his advice.

"Listen to the coaches," Gerald Ford, Sr., told his son. "Then, make your own decision."

Jerry made up his mind to talk with Willis. The black player was clearly hurt by the entire situation, but he did not hesitate at giving Jerry his thoughts. "You should play," Willis said. "We've already lost two games and we probably won't win any more. You've got to play, buddy. You owe it to the team."

Jerry was still deeply troubled, yet he knew Willis was right. When the Wolverines took to the field that day, they played with fresh spirit and life. When the final gun sounded, Michigan had defeated Georgia Tech 9-2. The only player to relish the victory more than Jerry Ford was a smiling Willis Ward.

Most Valuable Player

At the end of the 1934 football season, his teammates selected Jerry as the team's most valuable player. A special reward for his outstanding efforts was being selected to play in the Shriner's Crippled Children's Hospital game as part of the eastern squad. Jerry made the trip to San Francisco for the contest, held on New Year's Day, 1935. Of the 60 minutes the game took to play, Jerry was in for 56 minutes of the action. Although the East lost, 19-13, the thrill in just being part of the contest was substantial.

Pondering the Future

As his senior year drew to an end and graduation day crept ever closer, Jerry pondered his future. He had some professional football offers to consider, and the thought of money in his pocket was appealing. But he knew that direction would only lead so far. Economics and political science had been his major concentration at Michigan, so a career in law loomed larger and larger as a possibility.

The words of Abraham Lincoln –"It is as a peacemaker that the lawyer has a superior opportunity"– had always stirred a deep feeling within Jerry. Not every attorney was a bril-

*At the University of Michigan, center Jerry Ford captured
"Most Valuable Player" honors in his senior year for his prow-
ess on the gridiron.* (Gerald R. Ford Library.)

liant speechmaker or gifted orator; there were quiet mediators who worked in the background. But law school would cost money, and money was something Jerry Ford did *not* have.

AN OFFER FROM YALE

Once again, coach and friend Harry Kipke came to the rescue. Jerry had asked Kipke if there might be a coaching spot open on next year's Wolverine squad. "Maybe," Kipke answered, "but if I hear of anything else, I'll let you know." When Head Coach Ducky Pond of Yale University visited the Michigan campus, Jerry was invited to join Kipke and Pond for lunch. That led to a visit to the Yale campus in New Haven, Connecticut, for further discussion. Jerry was impressed with the atmosphere of scholarship and tradition which surrounded the eastern Ivy League school. The Elis were equally impressed with the respectful, quiet gentleman from Grand Rapids.

On the second day of his visit to Yale, Jerry received an offer to be an assistant football coach and also help coach the freshman boxing team. The salary would be $2,400 a year, a fortune to young Gerald Ford, Jr. The only problem was that he also hoped to attend classes as a law student. Could he do both? No, declared the deans of Yale Law School, the coaching position was a full-time job. Finding the coaching offer too good to resist, Jerry accepted it, planning to save all the money he could and then attend law school.

A Successful Season

Once he started his coaching duties in the fall of 1935, Jerry soon realized that he had made a wise decision. He would never have been able to study law while working; there were just not enough hours in the day. He enjoyed working with the young athletes at New Haven, and when Yale posted a 6-3 gridiron season, more than one player attributed some credit for the winning record to the new coach from the Midwest. In the meantime, Jerry budgeted his funds carefully, and he was delighted when he was able to repay, with interest, the $600 loan to the Congers.

Working at Yellowstone

The summer of 1936 gave Jerry a chance to head west again, this time to really experience the out-of-doors he had always enjoyed. Senator Arthur Vandenberg of Michigan helped Jerry obtain a job working at Yellowstone National Park. Directing traffic and supervising the campgrounds soon became part of Jerry's regular routine, but it was the feeding of the bears each day at Canyon Station that always proved eventful.

Giant dumpsters filled with garbage were emptied into an open pit, quickly attracting the smaller black bears from the nearby woods. Then the proud and ferocious grizzlies emerged to claim their rights to the scraps. This daily feeding ritual drew many spectators, and Jerry stood with a rifle in his hands on a flatbed truck not far away. If a grizzly appeared more interested in the onlookers and moved toward the people, Jerry was supposed to shoot. Thankfully, the only encounters were between the beasts themselves, and although he was always ready, Jerry never had to fire his weapon.

Making the Grades

In the fall of 1936, it was back to New Haven and another season of football. Yale boosted their record to 7 and 1, enough to win the Ivy League championship and place Clint Frank and Larry Kelley on the All-American team. For assistant coach Jerry Ford, his efforts earned him a $600 raise. There were some who suggested he should seriously consider coaching as a career, but Jerry had other thoughts in mind. He still wanted to become a lawyer.

Perhaps, Jerry thought, by earning good grades in a course or two he might convince the deans at Yale Law School to evaluate his potential again. So, during the summer of 1937, Jerry returned to Ann Arbor and enrolled in two courses, Criminal Law and Civil Procedure. Since he had been out of school for two years, getting back into the studying routine was not easy. Yet he managed to earn B's in both courses.

When Jerry showed his grades to Coach Pond at Yale, the coach agreed to allow his assistant to take law courses — as long as he did so during the spring term, when outside studies would not interfere with his football coaching. However, the officials at the law school were more dubious. Most of the law students at Yale had been honor students as undergraduates, posting far more impressive academic records than Jerry had. Nevertheless, sensing his eagerness and desire, the officials were willing to give Jerry a chance.

YALE LAW SCHOOL

The competition at Yale Law School was stiff. Many of Jerry's classmates not only boasted more impressive academic accomplishments, they had grown up in lawyer families and had already spent much time outside of school working in active law practices. Sargent Shriver, Cyrus Vance, Potter Stewart — all of these and others among Jerry's classmates were destined to make unique contributions to the legal profession after obtaining their law degrees.

But Jerry was not one to buck under the fierce rivalry for grades. After all, it was not only his own personal goal hanging in the balance but the honor of his family, the respect of three younger brothers, the faith of the Congers, and so many more people back in Grand Rapids who were rooting for him. He was one who worked best under pressure.

Romance Enters the Picture

The pressure increased when Jerry met Phyllis Brown, a co-ed attending Connecticut College for Women in New London. As a coach of the Yale boxing team, he would accompany the squad to New London for matches with the U.S. Coast Guard Academy. It was on one such trip that he met the attractive Miss Brown with the help of mutual friends.

It was the first serious romance for Jerry Ford, who had always been too involved with studies, jobs, and sports to have time for anything else. Phyllis Brown changed that. But in her junior year of college, she headed for New York City to become a professional model. Before long, her face was appearing on the best of fashion and glamour magazines.

Whenever they could find the time and opportunity, Jerry and Phyllis would get together. Skiing, golfing, going to the theater, playing tennis—clearly, the two were in love. Marriage plans were discussed. However, Jerry wanted to return to Grand Rapids and practice law there once he earned his degree. Obviously, there were few, if any, opportunities for Phyllis to further her own career in professional modeling if she went to Michigan. Despite long talks to resolve the matter, their relationship was doomed. Jerry and Phyllis agreed to split up.

STARTING A LAW PRACTICE

By January of 1941, Jerry had finished his law courses at Yale. He ranked in the top third of his class, no small achievement considering the caliber of his peers. Back he went to Grand Rapids in order to prepare to take the Michigan bar examination. A disciplined athlete and scholar, Jerry was accustomed to the pressure that preparation for the bar exam demanded.

Upon returning to Grand Rapids, Jerry was happy to find an old friend and fraternity brother from Ann Arbor, Phil Buchen, who was climbing the same ladder. Whereas most people in their situation might be searching around for established legal firms to join, Jerry and Phil were eager to start their own practice. And they did just that. As soon as they both passed the bar exam, the firm of Ford and Buchen was born.

Their first client needed a real estate title search. The matter was quickly executed, and a bill was sent out for $15. "Too much!" the client protested, so the two beginning attorneys reduced the bill to $10. That first earned $10 was a welcome sight to both of the young men.

Attack on Pearl Harbor

Word spread quickly about the earnest and honest Jerry Ford and Phil Buchen. Soon, people were coming in who needed help with pension trusts, divorces, and labor law violations. Each night the lights burned late and long in the Ford and Buchen office. The work was exhausting, but gratifying. Jerry felt important to the lives of the people around him. It brought him to the office early in the morning and he often worked 10-hour days.

One Sunday evening as he drove home after being at his desk all day, Jerry turned on the car radio. The news the tired lawyer heard made him become suddenly alert. Japanese planes had attacked the United States naval station at Pearl Harbor, Hawaii, that morning, December 7, 1941. There was no doubt what that meant—the nation would soon be going to war. Gerald Ford, Jr., was in for some drastic changes in his life.

Chapter 4

Battle Cry

It hardly seemed fair. Less than a year after starting their partnership together, Phil Buchen and Gerald Ford were splitting up. The last few months had not been easy ones, trying to attract clients in a city where businesses and industries utilized long-established legal firms to handle their affairs. The two inexperienced young attorneys were up against formidable obstacles. But because they handled those cases referred to them by local courts and other lawyers with all the dedication and attention they could muster, Ford and Buchen had already carved a small niche for themselves in the Grand Rapids community.

Now, those bombs that had been dropped so far away might well have fallen right on their practice. Jerry quickly finished up his cases as best he could. Then, at age 29, he joined the United States Navy early in 1942. Because of a youthful bout with polio, Phil Buchen was unable to enlist in the service. His legal abilities had not gone unnoticed, however, and he was invited to join the firm of prestigious local attorneys.

SEEKING ACTIVE DUTY

Jerry's naval career began first at Annapolis, Maryland, where he attended the U.S. Naval Academy as an ensign. He then went to the preflight school at Chapel Hill, North Carolina, where he served as a physical fitness instructor. His job was to whip into shape the hundreds of aviation cadets headed into active service.

Ford knew his assignment was important, but he longed to see action himself. His job at Chapel Hill was too much like sitting on the bench during a championship football game. Taking pen in hand, he wrote to every Navy superior he could think of. "I humbly request a service assignment that would offer more active duty in our war effort," he wrote.

Month after month slipped by. Then, in the spring of 1943, Ford received the answer he wanted. Orders arrived at Chapel Hill telling him to report to Norfolk, Virginia, for gunnery training, then to the *Monterey*, a light aircraft carrier, for duty in the Pacific. Not only was he given the tasks of a gunnery division officer on the *Monterey*, he was also to be the ship's athletic director. Someone in the Navy certainly knew how to put Ford's best talents to use!

First Combat

It was November of 1943 before Jerry had his first real taste of military combat. With the light cruiser *Enterprise* and six destroyers, Ford, on the *Monterey*, watched as U.S. naval planes blasted away at Makin Island in the Gilberts, then later pounded the Japanese base at Kavieng on New Ireland. It was a strange way to spend Christmas morning in 1943, standing on the ship's fantail and directing the crew of a 40-mm antiaircraft gun. Surely seeing the soft snow falling in Michigan and listening to carolers singing would have been a welcome change from the Japanese planes diving around them, their bullets and bombs ripping and exploding everywhere.

As vital as his position was, Ford still felt confined and restless as a gunnery officer. When the assistant navigator was transferred, Ford requested the job and got it. Now, when general quarters was called, he stood on the *Monterey* bridge and felt like he knew what was going on. It was a great feeling!

Attacking Japanese Islands

But the satisfaction of being more vital to the war effort was soon squelched by the ugliness of seeing friends killed and injured. Kwajalein, Eniwetok, Truk – such strange-sounding names of places so far away from the calm of Michigan. No sooner was the landing on one island completed, one battle waged, then there was another waiting.

The attack on Taiwan in October of 1944 promised to be fairly routine, but the schedule was completely disrupted when the enemy countered with a major attack from the air. Hour after hour the Japanese planes swooped low, their guns matching the blast from ships' artillery. Like thousands of others, a tired Jerry Ford carried out his duties, wishing for the end of the deadly struggle. When it finally came, the men aboard the ships let out a collective sigh of relief, then began preparing for the next encounter.

A Narrow Escape

After receiving new orders, Jerry Ford flew back to Grand Rapids for a brief leave. Then, it was on to the Naval Reserve Training Command in Glenview, Illinois. When his commander, Rear Admiral O. B. Hardison, offered Jerry an opportunity to attend the Navy-North Carolina football game at Chapel Hill, Ford jumped at the chance. It had been a long time since his own grand and glorious gridiron days, and this game promised to be a tight contest. Little did Ford know he would come closer to death going to see that game than he had during his years in combat.

The football game was scheduled to be played while Admiral Hardison was making an inspection tour of bases under his command. It was late on Friday evening before the airplane carrying the naval officials, including Jerry Ford, approached the runway at Chapel Hill. As rain pelted down, the wind jerked the craft around in the air.

Unfortunately, the small airport had no runway lights. The pilot, a former flier for Trans World Airlines, was not familiar with the runways at Chapel Hill, but he was determined to land his passengers safely. As the aircraft approached the field, the pilot suddenly realized he was headed for the wrong runway. This one was much shorter and had a different approach pattern. But it was too late.

His seat belt fastened, his hands gripping the sides of his seat, Jerry felt the plane pitch forward and careen down an embankment. It was halted by a patch of trees.

"Get out!" someone yelled. "This plane could explode at any moment!"

There was a mad scramble toward the exits, the escape hindered by the darkness of the night. Quickly Jerry jumped out of the craft, crawling and pulling himself up the small hillside. Only seconds after everyone was out, the plane exploded. Jerry was happy to escape with just the shirt on his back.

BACK HOME AGAIN

In 1946 after 47 months of service with the United States Navy, Gerald Ford, Jr., was glad to be back in Grand Rapids. World War II was over. He entered the Navy as an ensign and left with the rank of lieutenant commander. On his chest, he wore 10 battle stars; his service file contained many laudatory remarks from his superiors. "An excellent leader," noted one captain, while another observed that he was "at his best

Home from the war, Lieutenant Commander Jerry Ford shows his parents a map of the Pacific theater, indicating the voyages of his ship, the Monterey. *(Gerald R. Ford Library.)*

in situations dealing directly with people because he commanded the respect of all." Captain L. T. Hundt of the *Monterey* gave Ford a four-star rating, the highest possible.

As for Gerald Ford, Jr., he was only too happy to be able to observe Christmas at home with his family and friends in 1946. How grand the tree looked, how warm the house in East Grand Rapids felt. There was singing, presents, food, and the joy of being surrounded by those he held most dear.

Now it was time for Jerry to get on with the rest of his life. Phil Buchen was still around, working with the firm of Butterfield, Keeney and Amberg. Maybe they might have room for another associate. It was certainly worth a try.

Chapter 5
Into the House

War changes people. It definitely changed Jerry Ford. As a student and as a young lawyer, he had strong feelings of nationalism. While a student at Yale, he had written, "It is essential that the United States be totally self-sufficient, avoiding entangling alliances beyond its own borders. There is strength in independence; there is weakness in international involvement." These were the ideas of a political isolationist.

A NEW PERSPECTIVE

But being away from the United States while serving in the navy gave Gerald Ford an entirely new perspective of international affairs. Why *had* Germany and Japan decided to wage war? It was largely due to a thirst for power and a notion that other countries, including the United States, lacked the strength and resolve to stop any military aggression. That had been proven a gross miscalculation, of course, but there was little doubt that Germany and Japan took advantage of the military unpreparedness of unsuspecting nations. That, in the mind of Jerry Ford, must never happen again.

Although the German and Japanese war machines now lay mangled and beaten, other challenges could come along. Certainly the Communist forces were readily gaining strength. It would take "money, muscle and manpower" to help the battered countries of Western Europe rebuild now that the war was over, but it was equally essential that the United States be defensively ready for any potential aggression by an adversary.

Changes in Grand Rapids

War, too, had changed the city of Grand Rapids. In the past, the furniture industry had been the economic mainstay of the community, but now new businesses had come in, led by General Motors and auto parts manufacturers. Labor unions thrived as workers poured in from other states, especially blacks from the South. The city was growing, humming with new life and activity.

But whether or not there was room for Ford and Buchen to open a law office again was open to question. The two friends discussed the matter for a long time, then decided it might make more sense if Jerry tried getting a position with Butterfield, Keeney and Amberg, joining an established firm. Three hundred dollars a month was hardly a fortune for a typical attorney, but Ford's actual legal experiences were minimal and needed refreshening. The ex-serviceman was grateful to at least have a job, one with a law firm.

Getting Involved

Despite a heavy load of professional duties, Jerry also became involved in community activities. He joined the American Legion and Veterans of Foreign Wars, helped with the Kent County cancer drives and Red Cross campaigns. He helped plan local outings for the Boy Scouts and raise money for the United Fund. Through sports, he had made many black friends, often recognizing their economic, social, and political problems. Thus, it came as no surprise when he joined the local chapter of the National Association for the Advancement of Colored People (NAACP).

A New Interest

Life had fallen comfortably back into place for Jerry Ford. Even his younger brothers had married and were raising families. Now and then, when Jerry was asked the question, "When are *you* going to settle down?" the busy attorney gave more and more time to ponder the answer. When friends suggested that he take out Betty Warren, a fashion coordinator for a local department store, Jerry liked the idea.

But a telephone call to Betty was not received with much enthusiasm. She told Jerry that she was going through a divorce and the decree was not yet final. Anyway, she was busy with an upcoming style show. Never one to ignore a challenge, the eager attorney persisted. Utilizing his best legal techniques, Jerry made a case for himself, and soon he was seeing Betty Warren as often as their busy schedules permitted.

Jerry Ford's calendar grew more crowded each day. Not only was he handling routine assignments for the law firm, he was being requested by more and more clients coming in the door. Amiable, effective, organized, clear-thinking—Jerry's reputation was growing within the Grand Rapids community and beyond.

MOVING TOWARD POLITICS

Although active in many civic service organizations, Jerry was not satisfied with being just another name on a membership list. He wanted to make a contribution, to share his time and talents in whatever way would be most useful. It was only natural that Gerald Ford, Jr., would gravitate toward the political arena.

Grand Rapids, indeed, the state of Michigan itself, had been dominated by the Republican Party for decades. For years, political boss Frank D. McKay had run the state party machinery, but the war had brought about some changes. Younger Republicans were challenging the long-entrenched professionals and had made considerable headway. Nonetheless, some of the McKay cronies remained, not the least being Bartel "Barney" Jonkman, the congressman from Jerry's own Fifth District.

Before the war, Jonkman's strong isolationist ideas might have won favor with the Grand Rapids lawyer and his friends. But now Jerry supported President Harry S. Truman's efforts to rebuild European nations that had been ravaged by the war. Secretary of State George Marshall had designed a plan to help America's European allies rebuild after World War II. The Marshall Plan seemed a worthy way of pulling the world back together; it was supported by Michigan's senior Republican senator, Arthur Vandenberg. Yet Jonkman continued to criticize such efforts. "Let them do their own fixing up!" he insisted. "We've done our part."

Assessing His Chances

Jerry Ford took his concerns to a community political group called the Home Front, a group he had helped form shortly before the war intervened. As his friends listened, many agreed that Jonkman was certainly out of step with their thinking. But as a political target, the present congressman for the Fifth District was a formidable opponent. His ancestors were Dutch, as were many of the families living in the district. Having been elected before the war years, Jonkman had built up a firm footing in his position and would be a serious obstacle for any potential newcomer.

Nonetheless, there were those who thought the former serviceman and present Grand Rapids lawyer, "that fellow named Ford," might be just the underdog who could take on the veteran incumbent. Always liking a challenge, Jerry warmed to the possibility quickly, and decided to give it a try. Quietly, he and a group of political enthusiasts waged a campaign to assess his chances. It was essential that Jonkman not find out he might have an opponent, for to take him off guard would offer Ford at least a small advantage – the element of surprise.

Keeping his political plans from Betty Warren was a particular problem. After their first date in August of 1947, the two had continued to see each other frequently. Neither had considered their relationship all that serious at first, but within months both knew they were in love. Losing Phyllis Brown years before had been a painful ordeal for Jerry, and he did not want to be hurt again. Betty, too, wanted to avoid additional suffering, now that her divorce decree was final. But in their time together, in sharing their hopes and goals, Jerry and Betty realized how much they had in common.

THE 1948 CONGRESSIONAL CAMPAIGN

Jerry kept his political plans a secret, waiting until only a day before the official filing date in June of 1948 to announce his candidacy as congressman for the Fifth Congressional District on the Republican ticket. Surprisingly, Barney Jonkman seemed to care little about facing a primary opponent. In truth, the incumbent lightly brushed Ford's possibilities aside.

But when President Truman reconvened the 80th Congress and Jonkman had to return to Washington, Jerry saw his chances to make political headway. He scheduled speeches everywhere he could in the district. And when he did not have a speech scheduled, he stood at factory gates and on street corners to shake hands and meet new people.

"You probably don't know who Jerry Ford is," the eager challenger would declare at a country fair, "and you probably don't care. But by the time I've finished speaking, I hope you will." His directness, his sincerity, his good looks – all captured the attention of his audiences. They *did* listen.

A Maturing Political Philosophy

Campaigning became infectious. The more Jerry spoke, answered questions, and discussed the concerns of the voters, the more he liked it. He could not get enough. Slowly but steadily, his own personal political philosophy began to mature. "We can't solve the nation's problems by merely spending money," he asserted. Economically, he reflected the conservative attitude; however, on social issues he was more of a moderate. There were definitely areas that demanded financial support in the nation, but the money had to be carefully allocated.

As far as foreign relations were concerned, Jerry Ford was more liberal, recognizing the need for treaties and commercial ties with other countries. "America must work together, establishing contacts throughout the world, which will be of mutual benefit."

The difference in philosophy regarding foreign affairs was the major difference between Ford and Jonkman. In Washington, Jonkman ranted against the Marshall Plan and all other plans devised to rebuild foreign nations. The war was over, he declared, and the nation was obligated to remove itself from all entanglements beyond its own borders.

On the Offensive

Despite the fact that the majority of voters within the Grand Rapids community seemed to support the idea of less government rather than more, they also sensed a need for the country to take an active part in international affairs. Ford's message sounded clear and made sense. When Jonkman returned home after Congress had adjourned, he realized he had a strong opponent in Jerry Ford, who was waging a forceful campaign.

Clearly, the Grand Rapids lawyer knew what an effective offensive attack could produce, not only on a football field but also in a political campaign. Recognizing he had Jonkman on the run, Jerry challenged the incumbent to a debate. Jonkman declined. This did not sit well with the voters. In fact, it looked like the veteran congressman was afraid.

Next, Jonkman got into a series of disagreements with state union officials and press people. Then, when Senator Vandenberg endorsed Ford, it was a major victory for the challenger. When the primary was held, Jerry won by a two-to-one margin.

There was little time for celebration, however, because now it was the November election that demanded major attention. Granted, the Fifth District was heavily Republican, but Jerry Ford had played in more than one ball game when his team had been leading at halftime, only to come back for a demoralizing defeat in the second half.

WEDDING BELLS

But there was one thing that came first, and Jerry Ford refused to set that aside. On October 15, only two weeks before the general election, he married Betty Warren at Grace Episcopal Church in Grand Rapids. A few eyebrows were lifted as wedding guests noticed the groom's muddied shoes at the altar. But most knew that Jerry was campaigning every spare moment and he had probably cut a speech short just to be at the church on time.

Their "romantic" honeymoon that weekend included a drive to Owosso where the Republican presidential candidate, Thomas Dewey, was speaking. If Betty Ford was going to share Jerry's life, she might as well learn right from the start that politics were going to play a major part in it.

Jerry and Betty Ford flash winning smiles following their wedding on October 15, 1948, a day he called "the luckiest day of my life." (Gerald R. Ford Library.)

A political career begins, this one in a campaign quonset hut, as Jerry Ford runs for a congressional seat in 1948. (Gerald R. Ford Library.)

VICTORY!

As Jerry Ford cast his vote on election day—November 2, 1948—he was certain he had done everything possible to win. "The only bodies I didn't talk to in the past six months in this district are in cemeteries," he joked to friends.

As the results came in, the figures looked good. By the time the final tally was complete, Jerry had racked up 61 percent of the vote. It was a good feeling, a brief moment to celebrate the victory. But soon Mr. and Mrs. Gerald Ford, Jr., were packing their suitcases and heading east. There was a seat waiting for the fellow from Grand Rapids—a seat in the United States House of Representatives.

Chapter 6

Team Player

Jerry and Betty Ford surveyed the apartment they had just rented on Q Street in Washington, D.C. Plain, simple, nothing showy. But it would suit their purposes. It would have to. Jerry had $7000 in campaign expenses to pay off, and living on a congressman's salary of $15,000 a year enabled few luxuries. The newlyweds would be living on a tight budget, grateful for any help they could get.

FIRST TERM IN CONGRESS

At the beginning of his first term, Congressman Ford received some advice from a senior member of the House that proved more valuable than any salary increase could have been. It boiled down to two choices that every new Representative had to make — he could stay in his office and handle the business of his constituents back home, or he could spend his time on the House floor, watch everything going on, and become part of the Republican team.

Jerry decided to get the best staff he could to man his office, then devote himself to the action taking place on the House floor. He wanted to be an active member of the Republican team and make a difference in Congress. A Democrat, Harry S. Truman, occupied the White House, and the Democrats claimed a majority of members in both the Senate and the House. If the Republicans hoped to make a difference, even to have their voices heard, it was essential that they be unified.

An Early Political Lesson

But the eager, still naive Jerry Ford soon learned there were ugly sides of the political arena. One of his top assistants, recently graduated from law school at Catholic University in Washington, was a short, portly fellow by the name of John Milanowski. A Marine during World War II, John, like Jerry, came from Grand Rapids.

Since the Fifth Congressional District back home contained a goodly number of Polish Catholics, Jerry was convinced that John would be a useful liaison among those constituents. Not only that, before the war began John had taught public speaking, which was not Jerry's main strength. The new congressman could pick up some pointers from his assistant.

Without warning, before Ford's office in the House Building had even been cleaned up, letters started flowing in from back home. It seemed that some folks in Grand Rapids did not appreciate the new congressman's choice of a political aide. Newspaper editorials were critical too, warning Ford that he would never be re-elected if he did not get rid of "that Polack pope lover."

It was a major disappointment to Jerry to know there was that kind of narrow-minded thinking back in his home district. But when Milanowski offered to resign, Ford would not hear of it. "Don't worry, John," he told his assistant. "We'll kill them with love."

It was an early political lesson, not a very pleasant one, but a critical example of times ahead. So often there would be an immediate response back home to an action in Washington; then, within days, the entire matter would be dead. Milanowski remained on the Ford staff, constantly proving his worth. The two men remained very close.

Congressman Nixon

Another congressman, this one from California, caught Jerry's attention. Although not a powerful speaker, Richard M. Nixon always appeared to be organized, composed, and logical. He served on the Education and Labor Committee and on the House Un-American Activities Committee, both groups that were frequently in the public eye and capturing headlines.

Although Jerry received initial appointments to the House Subcommittee on Deficiencies and Civil Functions as well as the Subcommittee on General and Temporary Activities, he longed for committee appointments like Nixon had — committees that were affecting wider legislation and even engaging in controversy. As Ford and Nixon met on the House floor during debate, they exchanged thoughts and ideas. They became close allies, sharing similar political philosophies.

When Representative Albert Engel decided to run for governor of Michigan, Jerry got his chance at a "blue ribbon" committee. Engel had served on the House Appropriations Committee, a congressional group overseeing federal expenditures. When Engel resigned from the House of Representatives, Ford was tapped to take his place on the Appropriations Committee. It was a natural replacement — both were from Michigan and shared similar attitudes — but Jerry Ford felt fortunate to be chosen for such a key committee while still in his first term as a congressman.

Position on Issues

That first term slipped swiftly by, with Ford acquiring a good feel on how matters were handled in the House of Representatives. Politically, he seemed to take a moderate position, swinging to the conservative side on some issues, then taking a liberal stance on others. "There's a danger to becoming so rigid that you can never bend," he told his associates. "I want to keep an open mind."

Democrats and Republicans alike respected the new-comer from Grand Rapids. He was earnest and sincere, with a ready smile and quick handshake. His neighbor in the office next door, Democratic Congressman John F. Kennedy of Massachusetts, would frequently stop by for visits, and Jerry would often do the same.

UP FOR RE-ELECTION

In the fall of 1950, Jerry ran for re-election to Congress. Two years before, when he had first run, Ford had won 61 percent of the vote. In 1950, that margin swelled to 66 percent. It was clear that the people in Michigan's Fifth Congressional District approved of Jerry's performance.

It was just as clear that Jerry liked his job in the House. Someday, he hoped to be elected Speaker of that distinguished body. But that was a distant dream. For the present, Representative Gerald Ford, Jr., threw himself into the duties demanded of him by his constituents (the people of his district). For one individual, it might mean obtaining the rules and regulations required in establishing a small business. For another, it could be checking into the benefits due a World War II veteran. Or an elementary school student may want a picture and an autograph. As one day slipped into the next, Jerry would alternate his time between the House floor and his congressional office. But whenever he could, he would spend time with Betty.

A BOLD STEP

After Harry S. Truman announced he would not be a candidate for President in 1952, Jerry took a bold step in joining with 17 of his House colleagues to ask Dwight D. Eisenhower to champion the Republican cause. It was a somewhat daring move because Senator Robert Taft of Ohio was obviously the front-runner for the Republican presidential nomination and would little appreciate any opposition.

But Ford considered Taft too much of an isolationist. Eisenhower, a retired general who had not been involved in any previous political activity, offered the Republicans a fresh voice. In an exciting summer convention, Eisenhower beat Taft for the nomination and selected Richard Nixon to run as his Vice-President.

Jerry was delighted. But when the press accused Nixon of having a secret "slush fund" (campaign monies used at the discretion of the candidate), Ford became angry. He, too, had such a fund, and so did many other politicians. Yet Nixon was singled out and publicized, with illegal activity implied. However, despite the accusations and implications, Eisenhower and Nixon won a resounding victory in November, pulling in other Republicans on their political coattails.

A New Assignment

With the Republicans now a majority in the House, the party swiftly elected Joe Martin of Massachusetts as Speaker to lead the chamber. Jerry also received a boost, being named chairman of the Army panel on the House Defense Committee. Considering that his own personal experience had been with the Navy rather than the Army, Ford inquired about the selection. He sought out New York's John Taber, the new chairman of the Appropriations Committee, who had made the appointment.

"Sure, you've got friends in the Navy," Taber explained, "and that's why I put you on the Army panel. Friends sometimes expect favors, Jerry. I don't want to put you in the position of having to back away from your friends."

Avoiding Improprieties

Taber made sense. If Jerry Ford hoped to rise on the political ladder, it was essential that he never be tainted by a suggestion of scandal or even a hint of impropriety.

In 1954, when Jerry considered putting Betty on the office payroll – she was already fulfilling a variety of secretarial duties on her own – it was his assistant, John Milanowski, who persuaded him not to do it. "I know other Congressional people do it," the astute political advisor said, "and I know it's legal. But the people back home might misunderstand. Anyway, it runs against your entire philosophy of public service. If you need another office worker, look beyond your own family." Jerry agreed, and he was grateful that there were others looking out for him as he made various decisions.

Truthfully, despite her willingness to assist Jerry in any way possible, Betty Ford had plenty to do at home. In 1950, son Michael was born, and two years later, the Fords welcomed a second son, Jack.

Fear of a Senator

Washington became a true hornets' nest when Senator Joseph McCarthy began proclaiming in the early 1950s that virtually every federal agency and department had Communist employees. He claimed to have names and numbers, as people across the nation looked on and listened to his accusations. "Treason is with us!" the senator from Wisconsin thundered, and few wished to speak out against him for fear of being held open to suspicion.

Jerry and many of his political colleagues found McCarthy's accusations disgusting, even deplorable, but they did not care to challenge the man publicly. The fact that he did not do so haunted Ford for the rest of his career.

The longer Jerry Ford stayed in the House of Representatives, the greater his responsibilities became. He was appointed to a committee whose responsibility was the activities and expenditures of the Central Intelligence Agency. This federal bureau was established during Truman's administration to gather intelligence information about military activities in other countries.

DEVOTED FAMILY MAN

In March of 1955, the Ford family moved to a house on Crown View Drive in Alexandria, Maryland. It was a calculated move, based largely on the fact that each time Jerry ran for Congress, the voters of the Fifth District sent him back to Washington with a wider margin of victory than the previous election. Yes, Ford's position in the House was secure.

The move to a larger home was also necessary because the family was growing. A third son, Steve, joined the family in 1956. The next year, daughter Susan was born. With four children six years old and under, Jerry and Betty hired a woman named Clara Powell to help with family duties.

Despite a heavy calendar of political appointments, many taking him back to Michigan as well as to other parts of the country, Jerry was determined to fulfill his responsibilities as a father. Sunday was family day, and nothing would prevent him from being with his wife and four children. Sometimes it meant getting special flights and making special arrangements, but he did it anyway. The family would go to church in the morning, return home for a grand brunch, then simply enjoy games and conversation. Even when they did nothing, they were doing it together, and Jerry Ford considered that important.

Republican Changes

With Dwight D. Eisenhower as president, the Republican Party had a popular leader at the top. But Eisenhower was a grandfatherly type, projecting an older image. During his second term, when the country gradually slipped into a business recession and the economy seemed to be deteriorating, many people thought changes were needed.

In 1958, the electorate shifted gears and tossed many Republicans out of office, replacing them with younger, more energetic Democrats. No longer did the Republican Party dominate Congress. House Speaker Joe Martin was reduced to Minority Leader, and there were movements afoot within his own party to replace him. By January of 1959, that movement was successful; Charles Halleck of Indiana replaced Martin as Minority Leader.

THE ELECTION OF 1960

At the conclusion of Eisenhower's two terms of office in 1960, the Republicans had to find a man to take his place. The obvious choice was Vice-President Richard Nixon. Jerry Ford was surprised and flattered that some of the folks in Grand Rapids were pushing him as the second man on the Nixon ticket.

But Jerry had his own ideas about who should be the Republican candidate for Vice-President. He liked Thurston Morton of Kentucky. Morton had served in both the Senate and the House of Representatives. During the Eisenhower years, he had also served in the State Department. He seemed a wise choice, but Ford soon discovered that Richard Nixon had his own selection—Henry Cabot Lodge of Massachusetts, a former senator. A bit disappointed and yet loyal to the party, Jerry Ford campaigned actively for the Nixon-Lodge ticket.

The Democrats, sensing the national mood for youth and energetic spirit, picked John F. Kennedy, now a U.S. senator, as their presidential candidate. To balance the ticket geographically, Senator Lyndon Baines Johnson of Texas was tapped to run with him. Ford liked both Nixon and Kennedy, but naturally, party affiliation swayed his preference. In a very tight race, Kennedy was elected. Eight years of Republican White House control had ended.

Increased Stature

Despite losing the presidency, Republicans made substantial gains in the House and Senate. Jerry Ford's own stature increased because of his continuing service in the House and his seniority on the Appropriations Committee. This group carefully controlled the national budget and its expenditures for defense.

Because of his importance in the House, Ford was informed in advance of President Kennedy's intention to support a Cuban military brigade when it invaded Cuba in April 1961 to overthrow the Communist government of Fidel Castro. The Grand Rapids congressman was very disappointed when the mission failed. Because that failure was partly due to a lack of American air and naval support—support that Ford could have argued for in Congress—he accepted part of the blame for the mission's failure.

The Cuban Missile Crisis

Cuba was again in the spotlight in October of 1962, when an American plane spotted offensive nuclear missiles on the island. The weapons were obviously of Soviet origin. Ford and others directly concerned with national defense called for additional surveillance flights to collect indisputable evidence. When valid proof was obtained of the missiles' presence, immediate action was taken. President Kennedy demanded that the missiles be removed. When Soviet Premier Nikita Khrushchev backed down and told Kennedy that the missiles would be withdrawn, a major international crisis was averted.

A New Party Position

Since his first arrival in the House of Representatives, Jerry Ford had always gone out of his way to make friends. People had been good to him, and he returned the favor and passed it along to others. No one appreciated that more than new Republican members in the House.

In 1963, the younger Republican House members—"the Turks," as they were called—helped Ford take over the leadership of the House Republican Conference. It was an honor he deeply appreciated because the position gave him a policy-making voice in the Republican Party. He welcomed the opportunity, feeling that at age 50, he straddled the boundaries between the younger and older Republican factions.

INVESTIGATING AN ASSASSINATION

However, the joy of the new position within his own political party was quickly subdued on November 22, 1963. Jerry shared the grief of the nation when, on that date, President Kennedy was tragically cut down by an assassin's bullet in Dallas, Texas. Not only had Jerry Ford lost his President, he had lost a close friend as well.

At the request of the new President, Lyndon Johnson, Jerry was named to a commission assigned to investigate the Kennedy assassination. It was an assignment that offered little pleasure, but Jerry's selection to serve on the committee reflected the reputation of fair-mindedness that he had achieved in the nation's capital.

For 10 months Ford reviewed documents, heard testimony, and attended meetings concerning that tragic event in Dallas. John R. Stiles, a political advisor and friend back in Grand Rapids, assisted Jerry. The commission found that the assassin, Lee Harvey Oswald, acted alone and that there was no conspiracy. Later, Ford and Stiles would write a book entitled *Portrait of the Assassin* that would back up those findings.

Nonetheless, stories persisted that the Kennedy assassination was part of a conspiracy, that there was a cover-up, that the commission on which Jerry served had not found the truth. "There are always going to be doubters and skeptics," Ford noted, "and yet that is a freedom of our country—to question and challenge."

Chapter 7

Days of Decision

As the nation struggled to recover from the shock and grief caused by the assassination of President John F. Kennedy, his successor, Lyndon Baines Johnson, announced his program to push the country forward. Congress was swamped by legislation and spending bills, some part of "the Kennedy legacy" and others initiated by the new chief executive.

With his colleagues, Jerry Ford struggled to handle the massive amount of paperwork dealing with such measures as a major tax reduction, civil rights, a program to fight poverty, medical assistance for the elderly, and a federal pay hike. Each program and piece of legislation demanded careful study and analysis. It was important that the minority party, the Republicans, publicly challenge all proposals that were questionable.

In the House, Republican leader Charley Halleck attempted to win over southern Democrats in attacking some legislation, but the effort was largely in vain. A likable fellow personally, Halleck lacked the political charisma and dynamic qualities that could alter the flow of Democratic legislation. Many Republicans looked to 1964, a presidential election year, for possible change.

THE ELECTION OF 1964

Certainly, there was no shortage of Republican contenders for the nation's chief executive position in 1964. Barely defeated in 1960, Richard Nixon was clearly in the race. While employed by a New York City law firm, he was constantly working the Republican dinner circuit, calling for party "unity and strength." Governor Nelson Rockefeller of New York wanted the nomination, as did Senator Barry Goldwater of Arizona, who espoused a doctrine of domestic and international conservatism. From Jerry's own state of Michigan, Governor George Romney also expressed presidential aspirations. There was little doubt who the Democratic candidate would be — Lyndon Johnson.

District Redistricted

While politicians and pollsters debated the strengths and weaknesses of top potential candidates, Jerry Ford found his own name appearing frequently as a possible vice-presidential contender. Personally, he had little interest in the position. He still entertained thoughts of some day serving as Speaker of the House.

Anyway, there was talk circulating that the boundaries of all congressional districts in Michigan might be redrawn. And there was another rumor that all House members from Michigan would be elected at-large — that is, not from particular geographic areas but from the entire state. Because Democrats dominated in Detroit, this might snuff out Republican chances. However, when Governor Romney exerted some political pressure, the redistricting did not hurt Jerry Ford at all. He was confident he could win again.

A Comfortable Position

Governor Romney's desire to be the Republican presidential candidate afforded Jerry Ford a comfortable position during the 1964 Republican National Convention. While many Republicans were pressured to choose between supporting Goldwater and Rockefeller, Ford could defend his stance behind "the favorite son of Michigan." Romney's chances were slim at best, and convention delegates ended up nominating Goldwater. When he tapped William Miller of New York as his vice-presidential running mate, Jerry breathed easily.

President Johnson was virtually unbeatable, and Ford had grown accustomed to winning. Predictions of a Johnson landslide proved accurate, with Goldwater carrying many Republicans down to defeat with him. Not Jerry Ford, however. Once again he emerged unscathed by the political turmoil and was re-elected to Congress.

HOUSE MINORITY LEADER

For some time the group of Republicans in the House known as the young Turks had grown more and more disenchanted with the leadership shown by Minority Leader Charley Halleck. They wanted someone with more progressive ideas, more energy and enthusiasm, greater vision for the future. As the nation prepared to inaugurate Lyndon Johnson, House Republicans made a bold step of their own. On January 5, 1965, they elected Jerry Ford House Minority Leader by a narrow margin of six votes, 73-67.

Halleck proved to be a gracious loser, offering his assistance to Jerry at every opportunity. However, some of Halleck's supporters were very uncooperative, resenting Ford's victory. At times, Jerry found a changed mood on the floor of the House that was not always comfortable.

THE WAR IN VIETNAM

As the new House Minority Leader, Ford faced many crucial days of decision. President Johnson clearly had hopes of molding a "Great Society," a nation able to solve its own problems and care effectively for its citizens.

Unfortunately, America also faced a problem far beyond its own boundaries. The military might of the nation was heavily involved in a country in Southeast Asia called Vietnam, a land torn by Communist aggression. Money was needed to finance the Vietnam conflict as well as to finance the Johnson domestic programs, but the President stood firm on his promise not to raise taxes. Ford joined others in declaring that there just were not enough dollars for "guns and butter."

The Vietnam conflict soured more Americans each day. Surveys revealed that most people did not even know where the country was, and fewer still understood what American soldiers were doing there. Who started it? Who was the enemy—the North Vietnamese? The Russians? The Chinese? What did we hope to achieve, Americans wondered. Why couldn't we get out?

In Washington, Ford led the Republican ranks against President Johnson. Labeling the United States policy in Vietnam "a failure," he urged the destruction of Communist supply lines in the North. Furthermore, the new House Minority Leader served notice that the Republicans were tired of the chief executive and his top advisors expecting bipartisan support when no Republican suggestions were ever sought, no consultation ever requested.

The "Ev and Jerry" Show

If Republican opinion was not sought by Johnson and his aides, it was indeed shared in the media. Teaming up with Senate Minority Leader Everett McKinley Dirksen of Illinois,

In the mid-1960s, Republican House leader Jerry Ford joined the ever eloquent Senate Republican chieftain Everett Dirksen for a weekly media event, the "Ev and Jerry Show." (Gerald R. Ford Library.)

Ford became half of the televised "Ev and Jerry" news conference, where the week on Capitol Hill would be thoroughly discussed.

Dirksen, who might well have enjoyed a theatrical career had he not chosen politics, often stated that, "House Minority Leader Ford is the sword and I am the oil can." It was a fitting analogy, for while Ford often led a head-on charge against the Democrats and the problems in Congress, Dirksen came along behind, soothing and smoothing over the rough corners with consoling rhetoric and compromise. However, the two congressional leaders held differing views about Vietnam. Ford continued to criticize the President, particularly when he ordered periodic bombing halts, while Dirksen supported his longtime former Senate colleague.

THE ELECTION OF 1966

As the fall elections of 1966 approached, the hopes of most Republicans were high. President Johnson's leadership regarding the Vietnam engagement was being challenged in newspaper columns, at public debates, and in homes around the country. Opponents of the "Great Society" programs charged that the federal government was entering every nook and cranny of each private citizen's life. "Who will pay for all these new agencies, this increased legislation?" many asked. "Congress now is a pawn of the White House," asserted Gerald Ford in an October 1966 address in Cincinnati, "and 50 percent of the members are puppets who dance when the President pulls the strings."

There was little doubt that the Republicans would make substantial gains in the 1966 elections, and in the back of his mind, Ford wistfully fantasized about the possibility of a majority of Republicans in the House. With such a distribution, the Speakership would be within his reach.

When the voters went to the polls in November, the results revealed their discontent with many Democratic incumbents and the present administration. The Republicans wound up with a gain of 47 seats in the House—not a majority, but a sizable increase. Ford was pleased, although there was no chance of becoming the House Speaker—at least not this time.

Illness in the Family

But for the moment, Ford was more concerned about the health of his wife and mother. Troubled by a pinched nerve and arthritis, Betty was taking a heavy load of drugs to ease the pain. The demands of family and public life added to her responsibilities, and although she did not complain, Jerry sensed her suffering.

Back in Grand Rapids, Ford's mother had moved into an apartment following the death of Gerald Ford, Sr., in 1962. Dogged by high blood pressure and diabetes, she had endured the complications of cataracts (clouding of the lens in the eye), a splenectomy (removal of the spleen), and two heart attacks. Independent and stubborn, she pushed away efforts to slow her down. "You slow down and then you stop," Dorothy Ford declared. "That's not for me!" Nonetheless, her health and constant activity troubled Jerry Ford. (Dorothy Ford died a year later, in September of 1967, while attending a church service.)

Presidential Criticism

After the election, President Johnson unleashed a barrage of criticism at Ford personally, claiming that the House Minority Leader probably "played football without a helmet" and that he "couldn't walk a straight line and chew gum at the same time." Ford brushed the remarks aside, recognizing the chief executive's frustration over the Vietnam conflict. In fact, in March of 1968, Ford delighted an audience at the Gridiron Club by putting on an old football helmet he had worn at the All-Star game back in 1935. The flaps did not fit easily over the ears, causing Ford to remark that "heads tend to swell in Washington." The applause was deafening.

THE ELECTION OF 1968

That same month President Johnson stunned the nation by announcing that he would not run for another term in November of 1968. Clearly hurt by the criticism about Vietnam, he expressed a wish to leave political life behind him and retire to his ranch in Texas.

As usual, the Republicans were not without a number

of possible candidates – Nelson Rockefeller, Ronald Reagan, even Gerald Ford's name popped up now and then. But the front-runner was obviously Richard Nixon, despite earlier vows he had made to stay out of the political fray.

Turning Nixon Down

After the National Republican Convention that August in Miami Beach gave the nomination to Nixon, he then went looking for a possible vice-presidential running mate. He asked Ford directly if he was interested in the candidacy. The House Minority Leader thought fast. With 187 Republicans presently in the House and more surely to enter, thanks to the Democratic split over Vietnam, there was a good chance the Republicans might capture a majority. Just 31 additional seats would swing it. Then, the position of Speaker could be his. Politely, Ford refused. Richard Nixon went on to tap Maryland Governor Spiro Agnew for the second spot.

Weeks later, the Democrats met in Chicago and nominated Hubert Humphrey, Johnson's loyal Vice-President, as their presidential candidate. Ford liked Humphrey personally. They had come to Washington at the same time as part of the 81st Congress, and their families were friends too. When Agnew charged Humphrey with being "soft" on communism, Ford recoiled in horror quickly sending a note to the Republican vice-presidential candidate to watch his remarks. Ford was little used in the campaign, perhaps because of his criticism.

What appeared to be becoming a landslide victory for the Republicans slowed as the Democrats gradually got their own team working together. It was a down-to-the-wire finish on election day in November, with the the Nixon-Agnew ticket barely squeaking out a win. Sadly, especially for Gerald Ford, only five additional Republicans won House seats rather than the 31 he needed to secure the Speaker's role.

"That's politics," Ford told his aides.

Serious Misgivings

Having served as House Minority Leader under Democratic Presidents, where his job was to offer Republican alternatives, Ford looked forward to working closely with a chief executive of his own political party. Nixon's Cabinet choices were excellent people with considerable expertise.

But it was not long before Ford had serious misgivings about how effectively congressional matters would proceed. Neither of Nixon's two top aides, Bob Haldeman or John Ehrlichman, viewed the executive and legislative branches of government as a working partnership. Rather, the former branch gave the orders and the latter took them. There were certainly enough national problems, as well as the continuing Vietnam struggle, that necessitated combined leadership.

DISILLUSIONMENT AND GLOOM

The morale of the American public was very low. Thousands of people, especially college students, openly protested U.S. involvement in the Vietnam conflict, and many students even evaded the military draft. Nixon had campaigned on a promise to bring American soldiers home, and pressure to keep that pledge rose daily.

Ford himself, as chairman of the 1968 Republican National Convention, not only demanded a positive resolution to the Vietnam situation, but charged the nation to "rebuild our military power to the point where no aggressor would dare attack us." The assassinations of Martin Luther King, Jr., and Robert Kennedy in 1968 had also contributed to a general feeling of disillusionment and gloom.

Yes, the United States needed an injection of new self worth and pride, and Ford stood ready to assist Nixon achieve just such a goal. It was a time for decisions, but few could imagine the nightmares that loomed directly ahead.

Chapter 8

Riding the Rollercoaster

"Vietnamization." Such was the label given to President Richard Nixon's plan to conclude American involvement in Vietnam.

Ordinarily, following his election, a new President enjoys a period of grace with Congress, the people, and the media as he puts together his administrative team and formulates policies. But the fighting in Vietnam had dragged on and on, contributing heavily to the downfall of President Johnson, and now it was weighing just as heavily upon his successor. There seemed to be one unified cry, a plea to "End it."

Nixon's program of "Vietnamization" revolved largely around the immediate withdrawal of American troops with all fighting being taken over by South Vietnamese soldiers. In addition, Nixon's plan also included attacks by American forces on North Vietnamese bases in Cambodia, the major source of enemy supplies. Ford eagerly supported Nixon's policy, hoping that peace talks would soon commence.

ADMINISTRATION PROBLEMS

To many Americans, particularly those on college and university campuses, "Vietnamization" simply represented more war. Demonstrations broke out with President Nixon being condemned and even burned in effigy. At Kent State University, in Ohio, four student protesters were shot and killed by National Guard troops. "Is it not bad enough that we are losing our young people overseas?" challenged one angry newspaper editor in print. "Now must we kill them on our own soil? Are you happy, President Nixon?"

Richard Nixon was anything but happy. He pushed his White House staff and political colleagues on Capitol Hill to work even harder to move all phases of "Vietnamization" along with greater speed.

But foreign affairs were not the only area in which President Nixon was being criticized and putting pressure on his congressional lieutenants, such as Gerald Ford in the House of Representatives. Black leaders demanded an extension to the 1965 Voting Rights Act, initiated during the Johnson administration to make it possible for more blacks to vote. Nixon refused to give in to their demands, and insisted that Republican leaders support him in the matter. Despite many personal reservations, Ford agreed, convinced that loyalty to his President and political chieftain was of paramount importance.

Media Hostility

Seldom had the media ever taken such a hostile stand against an administration than it waged against the Nixon-Agnew duo. There was ample reason. Nixon had never felt fairly treated by newspaper and television reporters. At one point earlier in his political career, when he was considering giving up politics following a defeat, he stated that "now the press won't have Richard Nixon to kick around any more." Nor did his key aides, Bob Haldeman and John Ehrlichman, make any attempt to keep the doors of communication open with the press. Worst of all was Vice-President Spiro Agnew, who relished in lamblasting the network newscasters for their inept and biased coverage.

As House Minority Leader, Ford needed as much media support as he could get in order to muster backing for Nixon's programs. There were many days when he looked back nostalgically to when a Democrat was in the White House and the importance of the media was recognized.

Rejected Nominations

Nixon was even having problems getting his nominations confirmed. When a seat on the United States Supreme Court opened up following the resignation of Justice Abe Fortas in 1969, the President thought he would have little difficulty getting his nomination through Congress. He had already been successful in obtaining the confirmation of Warren E. Burger, a conservative from Minnesota, to replace retiring Chief Justice Earl Warren. To take Fortas' place, Nixon nominated U.S. Appeals Court Judge Clement Haynesworth of South Carolina. Nixon had promised the voters during the presidential campaign of 1968 that he would attempt to return the Supreme Court to a more conservative body, and surely Haynesworth was a step in that direction.

But a group of Haynesworth critics complained that he had shown unethical impropriety in some of his judicial cases, participating in arguments in cases in which he was directly involved. When Nixon was asked to withdraw the Haynesworth nomination, the President refused. The Senate then rejected Haynesworth 55 to 45. "Can't you talk sense to your chief?" one Republican colleague asked Ford. The House Minority Leader only shook his head and walked away.

Again President Nixon made a nomination to the Supreme Court, this time Court of Appeals Judge G. Harold Carswell of Florida. Although the Justice Department claimed to have thoroughly investigated Carswell, his critics quickly revealed that in 1948 the nominee had made a speech advocating white supremacy when he was running for state legislature. "I've changed," Carswell noted, but black leaders would have none of it. Legal experts and intellectuals pointed at Carswell's mediocre record as a judge, and 10 weeks after his nomination, he was rejected 51 to 46 by the Senate.

Investigation of a Supreme Court Justice

The Supreme Court was also on Ford's mind at this time, for many of the reasons that Haynesworth had been rejected. An investigation seemed to reveal that Associate Justice William Douglas was guilty of conflict of interest in certain cases brought before the Court, as well as receiving payment for improper legal duties performed.

The United States Constitution requires that Supreme Court justices serve only during periods of "good behavior." The more Ford looked into the Douglas situation, the more evidence he found indicating questionable behavior. Hoping for cooperation, Ford then went to the Attorney General, John Mitchell, for assistance. However, Mitchell proved to be a man of many words, more promises, but no follow-through.

Ford's investigation of Justice Douglas was moving slowly when, without warning, the Justice Department took a more active interest. When he finally had what he considered to be adequate evidence, largely because of the Justice Department's belated assistance, Ford went before the House and requested a special committee to investigate Douglas on five possible charges. When another representative introduced a resolution to impeach Douglas, that motion took precedence over any committee action. Ford had hoped to place his evidence in the hands of the House Rules Committee, but instead, it went to the House Committee on the Judiciary. After five months, a special subcommittee within the Judiciary Committee threw out Ford's charges.

Democrats, largely in political jest, accused Ford of taking action against Douglas in the House because the Senate had twice rejected President Nixon's Supreme Court nominations. Not so, claimed Ford. "I wanted to establish one standard for sitting judges as well as judicial nominees, to establish that there should not be a double standard on consideration of qualifications for sitting judges and those nominated later by a president."

It was not until June of 1970 that the judicial seat left vacant by Abe Fortas was finally filled. Harry Andrew Blackmun won easy confirmation, once again returning the Supreme Court to its full complement of nine justices.

Lifting Spirit and Pride

It was also in June of 1970 that Nixon's policies began to show some signs of lifting the spirit and pride of many Americans. The incursions into Cambodia were declared a "success"– a word seldom heard in connection with any event surrounding Vietnam. Three weeks later, the chief executive signed the extension of the 1965 Voting Rights Act and also lowering the voting age to 18. "For once," one university newspaper editor declared, "President Nixon has exercised a ray of fleeting wisdom in his office." A year later, the 26th Amendment to the Constitution, establishing the reduction in voting age, would become the law of the land.

A WEB OF SECRECY

Despite Nixon's steps to initiate international and national changes, political leaders criticized the web of secrecy with which he surrounded himself. Every 10 days, Ford and other Republican congressional leaders would go to the White House to meet with the chief executive, supposedly to exchange ideas and share opinions. But while the leaders of the president's political team in Congress provided open communication of the mood and attitude of the moment among their respective bodies, little information was forthcoming from the Oval Office. No one there was the least bit interested in consultation.

By 1971, communication between the White House and Republican members of Congress became virtually nonexistent. Yet President Nixon was able to inaugurate bold new initiatives in a variety of areas. He proposed direct diplomatic talks with both China and the Soviet Union. ("That's more than *we* get with the President!" one Republican leader jibed.) Presidential advisor Henry Kissinger then traveled to Communist China to make preliminary plans for Nixon to visit that country the following year. The President also announced the continued withdrawal of American troops from Vietnam, another 100,000 by December 1, 1971, and imposed a wage and price freeze in the nation, in hopes of stemming inflation. So much was happening, there was such a constant whirl of activity. Yet House Minority Leader Jerry Ford and Senate Minority Leader Everett Dirksen, who prided themselves on being "in the know," were often given only the briefest of details in order to explain the President's actions to their colleagues.

Congressional Criticism

A frustrated Congress began to criticize the President for not moving fast enough in ending the American involvement in Vietnam. That was, after all, one of his major campaign promises—he had indicated that he had a plan for immediate withdrawal—yet most Americans saw nothing more than a gradual pullout.

On the domestic scene, Nixon's economic policies were being regularly attacked. "He doesn't grasp the world of business," one Commerce Department official observed, "and there's sure no getting through to any of his advisors." To that, Jerry Ford could agree wholeheartedly. It was one thing to cautiously shield a chief executive from overextending himself publicly, but, largely through the efforts of Haldeman and Ehrlichman, President Nixon had become totally insulated. He was shielded not only from the country's general populace but also from those individuals in government, like Ford, who stood ready and able to do his bidding.

Opening New Worlds

As 1972 dawned, President Nixon opened the new year—an election year—with activities that ordinarily might have enhanced his image. On January 5, he approved plans for a space shuttle, recalling that mission in July of 1969 (during his term, of course!) when astronaut Neil Armstrong took that first triumphant step for mankind on the moon. "Our plans and programs must move forward," Nixon noted, endorsing the goals of scientists and space enthusiasts. "It is not only the world we know today, but the worlds out there which we must explore and better understand."

In February, Nixon was off to China, only a week after ordering a relaxation of restrictions on U.S. trade with that Communist country. Premier Chou En-Lai greeted the American President warmly, and live television carried pictures of the two leaders, always a smiling Nixon, around the world.

A short three months later, in May, similar pictures focused on similar scenes, only this time from Moscow, where Nixon was conferring with the Soviet leader, Leonid Brezhnev. As a result of this meeting, a space exploration agreement was signed on May 24 ensuring compatible docking systems on Soviet and American spacecraft. Two days later, agreements limiting Soviet and U.S. strategic arms were signed.

The Beginning of a Debacle

Despite his actions, President Nixon entered that politically crucial summer of 1972 with little personal and public popularity in the pre-election polls. Whatever he did, the chief executive seemed to be doing it for himself, for his own selfish goals, not necessarily for the good of the nation. Busily preparing for a visit to China himself, House Minority Leader Ford still spent much of his time defending the actions and motives of the President. In truth, Ford believed that Nixon was totally unaware of what his aides were doing in the name of the chief executive.

Politically, the President was a conservative, as was Ford. Yet both of them believed that the Republican Party was broad enough to include people of varying political philosophies. It had to be in order to survive. In 1964, in the presidential race against Lyndon Johnson, Barry Goldwater had attempted to narrow the party's political ideology and had suffered one of the greatest political defeats in the history of the nation. No Republican ever wanted that to happen again!

Then, in June of 1972 came news of the break-in at the Democratic headquarters at the Watergate complex in Washington. Another kind of political debacle was about to begin, and Gerald R. Ford would find himself right in the middle of it.

Chapter 9

A Time to Heal

Gerald Ford gave the Watergate break-in little attention or importance. Attorney General John Mitchell, head of the Committee to Re-Elect the President, stated emphatically that no officials in the Republican hierarchy had anything to do with the break-in. And on June 22, President Nixon himself told reporters at the White House the same thing. As far as the House Minority Leader was concerned at the time, the burglary was simply a stupid action taken by a few renegade, over-zealous Republicans. Unlike many other politicians in Washington, Ford was more likely to trust than distrust people.

ATTENDING TO MATTERS

Anyway, there were other matters to attend to, like a three-week trip to China. As a congressman, Ford had traveled overseas many times—to Vietnam, Japan, the Soviet Union, Western Europe, Korea—but never to China. Betty was also making the trip, as were Congressman Hale Boggs, the Democrat House Majority Leader, and his wife.

It was an exciting opportunity, and Ford was delighted with the chance to discuss ideas with Premier Chou En-Lai. The Chinese leader revealed himself to be intelligent, steel willed, and quite sophisticated. The two men were particularly concerned about the possible reduction in Soviet defense spending but neither one believed that would happen.

After returning to the United States, Ford entered Bethesda Naval Hospital for knee surgery, a longtime ailment dating back to his football-playing days at the University of Michigan. The operation went smoothly, and Ford was pleased to receive a get-well note from President Nixon saying, "We need you back in Congress as soon as possible."

THE ELECTION OF 1972

Congressional duties were not the only responsibilities on the calendar for Ford. Still limping from his knee surgery, in mid-August he again served as chairman of the Republican National Convention, which nominated Nixon for a second term. Nixon's choice as Vice-President was Spiro Agnew again, a man with whom Ford had little familiarity. Another note from the White House pleased Ford: "You looked so good on television while presiding that I became more convinced than ever you would make a great Speaker." But it remained to be seen if Nixon could pull in enough Republicans in the House of Representatives for this to come true. No one hoped for it more than Gerald Ford.

But it was not to be. Despite Nixon's major win over Democrat George McGovern, 521 electoral votes to 17, only 13 Republicans were added to the House membership, far from a majority. Party members grumbled that all the campaign efforts went to re-elect Nixon, while Senate and House races were relatively unsupported. A disappointed Ford, who had to beg officials of the Committee to Re-Elect the President for transportation to speaking engagements for candidate colleagues, was forced to agree. For his own part, Ford was easily re-elected by Michigan's Fifth Congressional District.

During the campaign, little attention was given to the June 1972 Watergate break-in. But despite repeated denials by President Nixon of any White House wrongdoing, evidence kept mounting that pointed to involvement in the affair by administration officials. Hearings into the matter conducted during the summer by a Senate committee added to Republican problems. Nevertheless, Ford remained convinced that Nixon was innocent. Perhaps he had been ill-served by some of his assistants, but certainly he was not personally involved.

AGNEW RESIGNS

In October 1973, at the height of the Watergate revelations, Vice-President Agnew was forced to resign. While he was governor of Maryland, Agnew had accepted financial kickbacks from contractors doing business with the state. Summoning top Republican leaders from across the country, Nixon sought their counsel. Their consensus: Jerry Ford was the man to replace Agnew.

Ford had already planned to run only one more time for his congressional seat, then he would quietly retire. Betty and he had already talked it over and agreed. But when President Nixon encouraged Ford to take the vice-presidency, the House Minority Leader—ever the party man, loyal to the team—accepted. After a rather smooth series of congressional hearings, Ford was sworn into office on December 6, 1973.

DOUBTS ABOUT THE PRESIDENT

Truthfully, Ford found the official duties of the vice-presidency easy compared to the busy, and often awkward, tasks he had been fulfilling as House Minority Leader. Presiding over the Senate, voting in case of ties, attending meetings—the pace

Vice-President-designate Gerald Ford confers with President Richard Nixon while Secretary of State Henry Kissinger and National Security Advisor Alexander Haig share top-level advice. (Nixon Project, National Archives.)

was considerably slower. But as the Watergate investigation continued to spread, and evidence continued to point to President Nixon's involvement in the entire situation, more and more people inside and outside of governmental circles were suggesting that the chief executive should resign.

In order to bolster Republican morale, Ford embarked on a busy round of speaking engagements. Unfortunately, he found himself in the position of trying to defend a man out of party and patriotic loyalty, for he was beginning to have doubts about Nixon's integrity.

It was revealed that many conversations in the White House Oval Office had been taped. After congressional investigators obtained the tapes, Ford was encouraged to listen to them. At first, he refused, but finally he was persuaded.

After he heard the tapes, Ford publicly claimed that there could be many interpretations to what President Nixon had said. Inwardly, however, for the first time, Ford began to have doubts about the President's honesty. He could no longer speak out in public defense of the chief executive.

THE PRESIDENT RESIGNS

By the early months of 1974, one word kept coming up again and again –"impeachment." In spite of condemning evidence from witnesses, on tapes, on written notes, President Nixon maintained his innocence concerning the Watergate break-in and refused to resign. While Nixon's staff hurried to prepare his defense in impeachment proceedings, Ford's staff made preparations to provide for a smooth transition into the presidency. Few believed Nixon could triumph.

Finally, on the evening of August 7, Nixon told his family and staff that he had decided to resign. Ford was summoned to the White House for a quick conference. The following day, Richard Milhous Nixon became the first U.S. President to resign from office.

ASSUMING THE PRESIDENCY

There would be no celebration for the swearing in of Gerald R. Ford as the 38th President of the United States. Neither the man nor the nation was in any mood for joviality. At exactly three minutes past noon on August 9, 1974, the oath of office was administered. Ford became the first American President to take over that position without having been elected to it or the vice-presidency.

A proud Betty Ford looks on as Gerald Ford is sworn in as 38th President of the United States by Chief Justice Warren Burger on August 9, 1974. (Gerald R. Ford Library.)

Initial Decisions

The Cabinet and White House staff were those of Richard Nixon. But the Watergate affair had already cleared out some of the staff members, including Bob Haldeman and John Ehrlichman. Ford was pleased that the White House chief of staff, Alexander Haig, agreed to remain, as did all the Cabinet members.

Ford's choice to replace him as vice-president surprised few people. Governor Nelson Rockefeller was a longtime Republican who represented a more liberal faction of the party. He would balance Ford's more conservative philosophy. But when Ford also announced that he would likely be a candidate for the presidency in 1976, more than a few eyebrows were raised. While being questioned about the presidency before he was confirmed as Vice-President, Ford had stated that he would *not* be a candidate for the presidency in 1976. Had a taste of the office changed his mind? Obviously, something had.

On the international scene, Ford sent messages to leaders around the world asserting that the policies in place during the Nixon administration would remain intact. Treaties would be honored, agreements kept. Not every country outside the United States understood how carefully structured the American system of government was, and Ford wanted no foreign leader misjudging the transferal of power.

A PRESIDENTIAL PARDON

While the voices of the rest of the world remained relatively quiet, the American public's demand for action regarding former President Nixon grew louder each day. People appreciated the effective manner in which Gerald Ford had taken over the executive branch of government. Nonetheless, there were daily editorials in the media insisting that Nixon be brought to trial for his abuses of powers while in office. Although he had escaped an impeachment trial through his resignation, countless Americans felt they had been lied to and their trust violated.

Less than a month after taking office, however, President Ford announced on September 8 that he was granting Richard Nixon "a full, free and absolute pardon." In Ford's mind, having to resign the presidency and then live with that humiliation the rest of one's life was punishment enough, certainly greater than serving any time in prison. Ford's decision was solely an act of conscience; he felt that it was in the best interest of the country. Nixon's health was not good, and his family had already suffered greatly. A trial might drag on for years. It was an ordeal that might kill the man, and Ford reasoned that the nation needed a time to heal.

The presidential family share a moment in the Oval Office after the swearing-in ceremonies on August 9, 1974. On each side of the President and Betty Ford, from left to right, are Jack, Steve, Susan, Gayle (Mrs. Michael Ford), and Michael. (Gerald R. Ford Library.)

Public Outrage

Public reaction to the Nixon pardon was swift. Government officials and private citizens alike expressed their outrage at Ford's actions. Most surmised that a secret deal had been made in advance – Nixon would resign then Ford would pardon him. In light of the political corruption that had been revealed throughout the Watergate investigation, the pardon seemed to be simply more of the same underhanded, devious shenanigans. "For a moment, Mr. Ford," chided one television commentator, "you almost had us believing that there just might be a speck of honor left in the world of politics, but now you have erased that hope."

Convinced that he had taken the proper course of action, Ford was shocked at the criticism. Even his own press secretary, Jerold terHorst, turned in his resignation. "If you're serious about running for President in 1976, you better hope the American people have a mighty short memory," one friend on Capitol Hill remarked. "You might have done what you thought was the decent and honorable thing to do with that pardon, but those folks wanted the whole story about Watergate, and if Richard Nixon was an instigator, they wanted him to go to jail." Gerald Ford could only shake his head. Clearly, this office would take some getting used to.

Amnesty for Draft Dodgers

But before the dust had settled on the Nixon pardon, the new chief executive became involved in another controversy. Wanting to heal the wounds from Vietnam and hoping to pull the people of the nation together, President Ford offered amnesty to all those who had been draft dodgers during that conflict. Again, there was a loud outcry, largely from the country's veterans' organizations. They were shocked that those who had avoided military service by fleeing to Canada should be honorably welcomed back.

Ford's amnesty pledge was conditional, however, in that those willing to accept it were required to complete two years of public service. This was not enough to appease the veterans' groups, but it did seem to pacify a large portion of the American people. Of 106,000 men eligible for the amnesty, only 22,000 ever applied for it.

CONTROLLING INFLATION

So much for looking back. Ford was eager to deal with present and possible future problems. There were certainly enough of those. Prices on numerous consumer items were raising constantly. This increasing inflation threatened to get out of control, sending the national economy into a tailspin. Upon the recommendation of key financial advisors, Ford set up the Council on Wage and Price Stability. The government could now exercise some control over wages and prices, hopefully easing the dangerous direction in which the nation was headed.

Another method of keeping prices down was to increase taxes. That possibility underwent careful study, but before any action could be taken, the economy slipped into a recession, an economic slump. Increasing government jobs of a public service nature and lowering taxes were suggested as a way to get out of the recession. To Ford, such actions made sense. Certainly, after some 25 years as a member of the House, he knew that reducing taxes had a more pleasing effect on people than raising them. The plan was passed by Congress with little difficulty, and by early 1975, inflation had slowed and the economy had recovered a bit. After the Nixon pardon aftermath and the amnesty outbursts, it felt good to enjoy a touch of public approval.

President Ford escapes the rigors and demands of his office as he hits the slopes near Vail, Colorado. (Gerald R. Ford Library.)

Investigating Federal Agencies

On January 4, 1975, President Ford announced that Vice-President Rockefeller would head a commission to investigate the operations of the Central Intelligence Agency (CIA) and the Federal Bureau of Investigation (FBI). Both were found to be implicated in the Watergate break-in scandal, and it was thought that their involvement could be a part of a larger pattern of illegal covert (secret) activities.

"It is imperative," declared Ford, "that the CIA and FBI be effectively and honestly used in the best interests of this country, never misused at the hands of misguided individuals." The subsequent investigation did indeed reveal evidence of serious misuse, leading to a restructuring of both agencies and a reshuffling of top key personnel.

FAMILY HEALTH MATTERS

On January 25, 1975, President Ford underwent a four-hour physical examination at the Naval Medical Center in Bethesda, Maryland. Shortly thereafter, the chief executive became the first President to release to the public a full report of a medical check-up. "He is in excellent health," reported Rear Admiral William Matthew Lukash. "The results of all medical tests were normal in every way."

Betty Ford, on the other hand, was not as fortunate. Only weeks after her husband took on the duties as chief executive, the first lady was diagnosed as having a cancerous lump in her right breast. Immediate surgery was dictated. If malignant, a full mastectomy (surgical removal of the breasts) would be performed. Hopefully, the cancer would be contained through the surgery. Throughout the fall of 1974, Ford kept a close watch on his wife's health, delighting in the realiza-

From the Shadows into the Spotlight

The historic events that catapulted Gerald Ford into the United States presidency also introduced the nation to a new First Lady. Elizabeth (Betty) Bloomer Warren Ford proved an immediate dramatic contrast to the woman who preceded her. Patricia Nixon had maintained a quiet demeanor during her years in the White House, seemingly caught up in the family affairs of her husband and two daughters. Although she performed the roles of her position, she clearly preferred a background seat and undertook no major causes of her own.

As a congressman's wife, Betty Ford had conducted herself in a similar fashion, her interest clearly focused on the well-being of her husband and children. She took no direct role in politics, preferring to remain in the shadows.

But as the wife of the President, Betty Ford assumed a more public role. Her earlier background proved quite useful in the spotlight as the country's First Lady.

Once a teenage model in Grand Rapids, Michigan, Betty Bloomer later became an accomplished dance instructor and student of Martha Graham. She attended the Bennington School of the Dance in Vermont and briefly worked with the Graham dance troupe in New York City. Returning to Grand Rapids, she became a fashion coordinator and a dance instructor for handicapped children.

Recently divorced from William C. Warren when she met Gerald Ford, Betty had also carved out an active life for herself as a working person. Following her marriage to Ford, she put her own career aspirations aside to become a wife and mother. As First Lady, she actively worked for the Equal Rights Amendment, emphasizing in frequent public speeches that "a woman is not a second class citizen, but she should enjoy all the rights and freedoms of every American."

Not only did she play an active role in the campaign for women's rights, Betty Ford also worked actively in behalf of the fine arts and handicapped children. "If we fail to recognize the potential of boys and girls who are supposedly handicapped," she observed, "we will find ourselves far more handicapped than they might ever be."

When she was diagnosed as having breast cancer, Betty Ford chose to publicly share the rigors of a mastectomy in late September of 1974. The openness and candor with which she endured the operation was credited with encouraging countless women to seek medical examinations and advice concerning the disease. Her subsequent struggles with drug and alcohol dependency continued to spotlight such problems among all levels of society. "There are some who feel I have been too public with the personal struggles in my life," Betty Ford has stated, "but if my own difficulties have helped anyone else, I'm glad."

There is no question that the Betty Ford Foundation, established in 1982 and maintained for those people suffering from drug and alcohol dependency, continues as a living legacy to a woman who chose to make her own personal problems public in an effort to help others. Film actress Elizabeth Taylor, herself a former patient at the foundation, credits the staff and treatment with providing her "with a new life, a life containing richer perspective and strength." Other patients, the famous and obscure, echo the movie star's sentiments, a lasting tribute to Betty Ford's contributions and courage.

tion that the cancer was arrested and her subsequent recovery proceeded smoothly.

As for Betty, she refused to hide anything from the public. She was particularly pleased to learn about the increase in women having physical examinations at cancer clinics. "You see, I can make a contribution even from a hospital bed," she joked to reporters, as a proud President looked on.

FOREIGN AFFAIRS

Ford soon came to appreciate the secretary of state he had inherited from the Nixon administration. Although arrogant and not always a media pleaser, Henry Kissinger, who had been Nixon's national security advisor, had a firm grasp on foreign affairs and stood ready to do whatever was necessary to maintain the U.S. position in dealing with other nations.

When Ford sensed it might be useful for Kissinger to cool tensions in the Middle East, off the secretary of state went. To keep open the discussions going on with the Soviet Union, Kissinger flew to Moscow.

But there was little glory in the withdrawal of U.S. troops from Vietnam, and the countless numbers of refugees leaving that country posed even more problems. As the Americans left Southeast Asia, the South Vietnamese soldiers who replaced them were no match for the North Vietnamese. By the end of April 1975, Saigon, the capital of South Vietnam, was in the hands of the Communists. President Ford knew that other foreign countries were wondering what future events might challenge the strength of the United States against adversity, and how the nation would respond.

The *Mayaguez* Incident

There was no need to wonder for long. In Cambodia (now Kampuchea), the Communist Khmer Rouge forces detained an American merchant ship, the *Mayaguez*, in international waters. Since there was no officially recognized government in that Asian nation, there was no one to whom to protest. Was it an act of piracy? Was it an act of war? No one seemed to have the answer, but one point was clear—immediate action was necessary.

Thirty-nine American crewmen were on board the *Mayaguez*, and the world was watching. Under the War Powers Act, the President has the fight to authorize a military rescue when he considers such action necessary. President Ford informed Congress of his plans, then ordered such a rescue. A Marine invasion force managed to free the crewmen and their ship, but at the cost of 41 American lives. The loss of life troubled Ford, who believed the operation had been poorly executed. But the world saw that the United

States would not be pushed around and would fight back if challenged.

Attracting Little Attention

The *Mayaguez* incident offered high-level drama in an administration that had witnessed little exciting activity during its first eight months. Fulfilling earlier promises made by former President Nixon, Ford made brief visits to Japan, Korea, and even the Soviet Union. Although he emphasized that as long as he was President, the United States would honor any and all commitments overseas, Ford's remarks and movements attracted no particular headlines or major notice. Never did he master the art of a catch phrase that would be remembered or a gesture with which he could be immediately associated.

Nor did Ford's efforts on the home front to free Americans from the federal bureaucracy that had been so greatly increased by President Johnson's "Great Society" win any special recognition. And despite the fact that efforts to fight inflation continued to show positive results, these, too, garnered little public attention.

Then, on May 31, 1975, President Ford stumbled into international headlines quite unintentionally. In only a few fleeting seconds, he managed to leave a personal impression in people's minds around the world, an impression that would haunt the rest of his administration and perhaps the rest of his life.

Chapter 10
Russian Roulette

It happened in Austria, at the Salzburg airport. Fresh from an appearance and speech before the members of the North Atlantic Treaty Organization (NATO) in Brussels, Belgium, and a meeting in Spain to discuss American military bases in that country, Ford arrived in Salzburg for a meeting with Egypt's President Anwar Sadat. Rain clouds threatened, causing Ford to cautiously grab an umbrella in his left hand as he departed *Air Force One,* the presidential plane. His right hand was around his wife's waist. When he was only a few steps from the bottom of the ramp, the heel of Ford's shoe caught on something and he fell to the tarmac below. Immediately, he was back on his feet, a bit embarrassed but uninjured.

A DAMAGING IMAGE

Sadly, that minor incident came back to haunt Ford again and again. The delicate negotiations with Sadat regarding an Egyptian-Israeli crisis went virtually unnoticed. Instead, the world witnessed the President of the United States falling on his face. "Is he sick?" reporters asked. "Exhausted?" queried others. No, he had simply tripped and fallen, an accident that could happen to anyone.

However, the incident lingered in the minds of many,

and the subsequent re-enactments and jibes by television comedians and in newspaper cartoons constantly reminded the American people of the event. From that moment on, the media highlighted Ford falling in the snow while skiing, hooking a golf shot on the links, or any other fumbling or stumbling action. It was hardly an image helpful to the leader of a great nation, and would later prove to be politically damaging in his campaign for re-election.

FIGHTING CRIME

On his return to Washington from Salzburg, Ford spoke out against crime, a growing issue in the country. In a message to Congress, the President noted: "For too long the law has centered its attention more on the rights of the criminal than on the victim of crime. It is high time we reverse this trend." He suggested mandatory prison terms for those who committed federal offenses with firearms or other dangerous weapons, and the same for drug traffickers, airplane hijackers, and kidnappers. Ford argued that fines and prison terms should fit the seriousness of the crime. Too often, he said, fines were woefully low and did nothing to deter those whose business was crime. Although he opposed federal regulation of guns or the licensing of gun owners, Ford advocated banning the manufacture and sale of "Saturday night specials," weapons used almost solely for criminal purposes.

In the realm of business crime, Ford recommended that maximum fines for individuals found guilty of corporate offenses be increased to $100,000, while an organization or business might pay up to $500,000. Additionally, he warned big business interests that the attorney general would be directing more attention to exposing and prosecuting corporate abuses.

RUNNING FOR THE PRESIDENCY

As he was preparing to officially announce his plans to run for the presidency in 1976, Ford received good news from his economic advisors. Over the preceding six months, the inflation rate had dropped from 12 percent to six percent. Apparently, Ford's anti-inflation tax program—a temporary five percent surcharge on corporate and upper level incomes, a reduction of taxes on lower level incomes, tax credits for investments, the liberalization of the capital gains tax—all were working to achieve the desired end, a more stable national economy. Even the unemployment rate, 9.2 percent during May 1975 was declining. With luck, by 1980 there could be a budget surplus of $22 billion. Ford's WIN campaign (Whip Inflation Now!) seemed to be doing just that.

Ford had once promised to retire from politics in 1977, but since making that decision, the situation had changed greatly. He now felt needed by the country. His family, especially Betty, agreed, and they encouraged him to seek the presidency in the 1976 campaign. On July 8, 1975, President Ford announced his decision: "I expect to work hard, campaign forthrightly and do the very best I can to finish the job I have begun."

As to possible Republican challengers in the presidential primaries, Ford aides believed that Ronald Reagan would pose the greatest threat. In his eight years as governor of California, Reagan had mounted a strong conservative base of support, seemed to be knowledgeable about many issues far beyond his own state, and had transformed a movie image into a charismatic political figure.

However, in Ford's view, Reagan's thinking was too simplistic; he did not analyze a problem from many angles. Also, the California governor always believed he was right; he would seldom acknowledge a mistake. Nor was he a hard worker physically, preferring a less demanding schedule than the presidency requires. From personal experience, Ford recognized the liabilities of all of these attributes.

A CONTROVERSIAL CONFERENCE

At this point in time, however, campaigning would have to wait while Ford attended to more important matters. In only a few weeks, he would be going to Helsinki, Finland, to attend a 35-nation conference on security and cooperation in Europe. It was a controversial mission. Many American political leaders, including Ronald Reagan, were totally opposed to the President attending the meeting because most believed nothing useful would come of it, particularly for the United States.

As noble as the meeting's goal sounded—to have all nations attending the conference sign documents that spelled out their commitments in the areas of military security, cultural and economic cooperation, and the freedom of movement and expression of ideas—most people were wary of sending a President with only a year's experience to such a gathering. They were especially concerned about Ford meeting face-to-face with Soviet Premier Leonid Brezhnev.

An Optimistic President

President Ford, however, was more optimistic. It would not be his first encounter with the formidable Russian adversary. In meetings held in the Soviet Union in November 1974, Ford had fared well with the "opposition" although little concrete had come out of their discussions, largely because of major differences about weapons.

Ford welcomed a chance to meet again with Brezhnev

in Helsinki. "Doors of communication must always be kept open," he told reporters at the White House. "One cannot talk through locked doors, or when one refuses to visit another's doorstep."

But Ford's critics were dubious. In reference to the earlier incident in Austria, one notable Republican leader mumbled, "There's a good chance the world is going to watch our chief executive fall on his face once again. In any case, we should not be playing Russian roulette when the opponent has loaded the pistol."

Off to Helsinki

Despite the moans and groans, Ford took off from Washington and headed across the Atlantic. Stops were planned in West Germany and Poland before going to Finland. After the meeting in Helsinki, Ford also visited Romania and Yugoslavia. The countries he visited were carefully selected. Ford wanted to solidify U.S. relations, economically and militarily, with Chancellor Helmut Schmidt of West Germany. And it could certainly do no harm to encourage the independence of the three countries that seemed to be the least Communistic in the Soviet bloc of Eastern European nations.

Betty and son Jack accompanied President Ford, with the ever-present Henry Kissinger close at hand. Once in Helsinki, the tough negotiations began, with Andrei Gromyko, the Soviet ambassador to the United States, assisting the stern and wily Brezhnev.

The conference started with the Russians expressing annoyance with the American handling of the crisis in the Middle East, claiming that the Soviet Union was not being included in the peace process between the Israelis and the Palestinians. Such accusations were countered in kind by the United States. Then, when discussions concerning underground nuclear tests and certain strategic weapons became deadlocked, the first session was adjourned and arrangements were made to meet again.

An Eloquent Speech

Before the second meeting, Ford had an opportunity to address the other heads of state attending the Helsinki conference. He welcomed the chance. Speaking with unusual eloquence and deliberation, he said:

> . . . Peace is not a piece of paper. But lasting peace is at least possible today because we have learned from the experience of the last thirty years that peace is a process requiring mutual restraint and practical arrangements. This conference is a part of that process — a challenge, not a conclusion. We face unresolved problems of military security in Europe; we face them with very real differences in values and aims. But if we deal with them with careful preparations, if we focus on concrete issues, if we maintain forward movement, we have the right to expect real progress.

Ford paused, then looking directly at Leonid Brezhnev so his words would not be misunderstood, he continued:

> To my country, these principles are not clichés of empty phrases. We take this work and these words very seriously. We will spare no effort to ease tensions and to solve problems between us, but it is important that you realize the deep devotion of the American people and their government to human rights and fundamental freedoms and thus to the pledges that this conference has made regarding the freer movement of people, ideas, information. History will judge this conference not by the promises we make but by the promises we keep. Our people want a better future. Our presence here offers them further hope. We must not let them down.

After their meeting in Helsinki, President Ford and Soviet General Secretary Leonid I. Brezhnev met later in Vladivostok, USSR, where they signed a joint communique following talks to limit strategic offensive arms. (Gerald R. Ford Library.)

The media lauded President Ford's remarks. And he, too, felt that he had carried a clear message to the leaders and the people of Europe and the rest of the world. But if he hoped his speech had changed the direction of the strategic arms limitation talks (SALT) with the Soviet Union, he was in for a big disappointment. Because Brezhnev remained stubborn and unyielding, Ford and Kissinger would not change their positions. There would be no formal agreements at Helsinki concerning arms limitations, only the decision for top officials to continue discussions later in the year.

DECLINING POPULARITY

Ford returned home satisfied as to the overall success of the Helsinki mission, but disappointed that no major break-throughs had occurred. The Russians, however, soon began a successful public relations campaign. They claimed that Ford and Kissinger had "sold out" America in Finland by agreeing to accords that were contrary to the best interests of the Allies in Europe and by bending to a strong and prudent Soviet presence at the conference. Ford's satisfaction of the Helsinki meeting plummeted, as did his popularity according to public opinion polls.

As if that was not enough, there was grumbling within the Republican Party about whether or not Nelson Rockefeller should remain on the ticket in 1976 as the vice-presidential candidate. Strong conservatives resented his presence and considered him a liability; others argued in his behalf. Ford himself appreciated the work Rockefeller had done as Vice-President.

Critics Galore

Then there were those who complained that Ford had not expressed an open and warm public welcome to exiled Soviet author Aleksandr Solzhenitsyn, who had recently come to America. A belated invitation to the White House was not enough to appease many critics, and Solzhenitsyn was now reported to be too busy to come. "It would have been a wonderful opportunity for Ford to have demonstrated the hospitality of the nation," noted one newspaper editorial, "but the President muffed his chance."

According to many, Betty Ford also muffed things when interviewed by CBS reporter Morley Safer on the popular television program "60 Minutes." Asked if her children had tried marijuana, the First Lady calmly answered, "Probably." That same answer was given when she was asked if she would have tried it herself had marijuana been in vogue when she was younger.

Two Close Calls in One Month

Four times in the course of U.S. history, assassins' bullets have cut down American Presidents while in office. Abraham Lincoln was the first in 1865, followed by James Garfield in 1881, William McKinley in 1901, and John F. Kennedy in 1963. During the month of September 1975, President Gerald Ford was the target of assassins on two separate occasions.

The first assassination attempt took place a short distance from the California State Capitol in Sacramento on September 5. Lynette Alice Fromme, known as "Squeaky," pointed a loaded pistol at President Ford as he moved through a crowd. A quick-thinking and agile Secret Service man, Larry Beundorf, jammed his hand over the .45-caliber gun, preventing the weapon from discharging. In a later examination, it was discovered that the weapon's bullet chamber was empty.

Fromme, 27, was found to be a devoted follower of convicted murderer Charles Manson. Charged with attempted assassination, Fromme was tried in U.S. District Court and found guilty. She was given a life sentence.

Less than three weeks later, on September 22, 45-year-old Sara Jane Moore fired a single shot at President Ford as he left the St. Francis Hotel in San Francisco. The bullet missed the chief executive by some five feet, hitting instead a taxi driver nearby. Moore was quickly disarmed and arrested.

*President Ford is surrounded by secret security officials follow-
ing an attempt on his life in Sacramento, California, on September 5, 1975.* (Gerald R. Ford Library.)

A subsequent investigation revealed that
Moore had been arrested for carrying an illegal handgun only one day before the shoot-
ing. The weapon was confiscated, but Moore
was released. Active in radical political groups
at the Berkeley campus of the University of
California, Moore had been employed as an
informant by the Federal Bureau of
Investigation.

When Moore appeared at the U.S. District Court in San Francisco, she entered a guilty plea. The plea was accepted and she received a life sentence.

Despite the two attempts on his life, President Ford refused to be intimidated. He told reporters:

> I don't think any person as President ought to cower in the face of a limited number of people who want to take the law into their own hands. The American people want a dialogue between them and their President and their other public officials. And if we can't have that opportunity of talking with one another, seeing one another, shaking hands with one another, something has gone wrong in our society. I think it's important that we as a people don't capitulate to the wrong element, an infinitesimal number of people who want to destroy everything that's best about America.

About the recent Supreme Court decision to legalize abortions, Betty declared, "It's the best thing in the world, a great, great decision." Immediately the White House was bombarded with phone calls and letters, most critical of Betty's opinions on abortion. "She's entitled to her views," a loyal husband declared.

A NEW ECONOMIC PROGRAM

Although the nation's economy seemed to be stabilizing, Ford and his financial advisors saw possible economic problems ahead for fiscal years 1976 and 1977. To keep the federal budget below $400 billion, something had to be done. So Ford went on television on October 6, 1975, and proposed some immediate and surprising action.

In Ford's words, the American people had a choice between "bigger government, higher taxes and higher inflation" or "a new direction, bringing to a halt the momentous growth of government, restoring our prosperity and allowing each of you a greater voice in your own future." Emphasizing the need for the latter choice, Ford proposed "a substantial and permanent reduction in our federal taxes, and second, that we make a substantial reduction in the growth of our federal spending."

Democrats immediately attacked the program, claiming that such valued and necessary areas as veterans' pensions, food stamps, and Social Security could not be maintained if taxes were reduced. But the overall reaction to Ford's plan was extremely favorable.

Ford appeared ready to manage the federal budget, but he wanted little part of the requests from New York City and state officials to bail that metropolis out of its financial woes. The U.S. government was already supplying 25 percent of the city's budget through welfare assistance, Medicaid, food stamps, and other programs. Despite persistent pleas, Ford turned a deaf ear: "The federal government cannot answer to a city, any city, when such financial problems arise."

TEAM CHANGES

Secretary of Defense James Schlesinger seemed determined to cause problems for the presidential team. He had to go, and Ford knew it. Schlesinger fought with Congress, challenged Kissinger, and generally refused to support the ways and means of achieving administration goals.

A new image was needed for the Central Intelligence Agency too, although the present director, William Colby, had served the agency well. It was a matter of public impression because investigations had revealed that the CIA needed reorganization and restructuring, starting at the top.

Ford also wanted Henry Kissinger to wear but one hat, that of secretary of state, and to remove the second, that of national security advisor. And with the poor health of Rogers Morton, the secretary of commerce, Ford needed a new man in that department. The position was offered to and accepted by former Attorney General Elliot Richardson, who had resigned that post during the Nixon–Watergate turmoil. The Ford team was changing, and Nelson Rockefeller's decision not to be on the ticket for the 1976 elections necessitated still another change.

The personnel changes in Ford's administration caused another barrage of criticism from the media. Schlesinger had enjoyed a "hard-line" image among conservatives, and they denounced the change. Others in the liberal camp bemoaned the loss of Rockefeller. Columnist Joseph Kraft quipped that the shifts "stimulated new doubts as to whether Ford has the brains to be President."

Grain for Russia

While Ford endured the political brickbats for his administrative changes, at least one problem was resolved. American farmers, encouraged to increase grain production in the spring of 1975, had boasted a record yield. However, a complicated turmoil involving American farm organizations, Soviet wheat and seed-grain purchases from the United States, and the refusal of the longshoremen's union to load grain on ships destined for the Soviet Union caused Ford to reluctantly declare a moratorium on grain exports to Russia. But after weeks of negotiation, the problems were resolved, and by the end of October 1975, longshoremen were again loading grain for shipment to the Soviet Union. This made the farm organizations and the farmers quite content with a five-year grain contract that had been negotiated with the Russians.

A Conference in France

In November, Ford flew to Rambouillet, France, for an international economic conference with French President Giscard, West German Chancellor Helmut Schmidt, British Prime Minister Harold Wilson, and others. The atmosphere was congenial, with a consensus that all countries involved should share a clear understanding of each other's monetary, trade, and general economic policies.

Ford felt comfortable and at home in the meetings. Some of the leaders expressed interest in Secretary of State Kissinger's planned visit to Moscow in December. No one had higher hopes than Ford that progress toward a SALT agreement would be achieved.

A Supreme Court Appointment

On November 12, Associate Justice William Douglas notified Ford that he would be leaving the Supreme Court because of ill health. For 36 years Douglas had been a member of that distinguished judicial body, and although Ford did not personally support many of the justice's legal opinions, he was most sincere when he expressed the thanks of his countrymen for Douglas' many years of service.

Discussing a possible replacement with the attorney general, Ford asked for names to be considered, emphasizing that women were not to be excluded. The chief executive wanted to avoid the snags that befell Nixon with his nominations of Haynesworth and Carswell. Judge John Paul Stevens of the U.S. Court of Appeals in Chicago emerged as the strongest candidate. He was subsequently confirmed by the Senate, 98 to 0.

BACK TO CHINA

In late November, President Ford went to the People's Republic of China for the second time. In his previous visit in 1972, Ford had met with Premier Chou En-Lai. Because Chou was now dying of cancer in a Beijing hospital, Communist Chairman Mao Tse-Tung and the newly designated Vice-Premier, Deng Xiao Ping, were the official hosts.

At 82, Mao Tse-Tung was also clearly ailing physically, yet his mind was alert and he could express his feelings without hesitation. In a discussion with Ford, Mao focused his remarks around the need for the United States to stand up to the threat of Soviet domination around the world. Ford left the meeting keenly aware that the People's Republic of China, at least under Mao and his colleagues, would do everything possible to destroy any grip that the Soviet Union might have in Asia.

In the days that followed, Ford and Vice-Premier Deng discussed means of normalizing diplomatic relations as well as ongoing activities with Taiwan, the "other" China. Deng showed a pragmatic approach, was obviously a "doer" as well as a thinker, and displayed an amazing understanding of world affairs.

A TASTE OF THINGS TO COME

The U.S. ambassador to the People's Republic of China at that time was George Bush, who was Johnny on the spot at each session. Already impressed with Bush, Ford felt he would make a fine choice as the new director of the Central Intelligence Agency, to which Bush agreed. Immediately upon his return to Washington, Ford submitted Bush's name to Congress.

President Ford and Vice-Premier Deng Xiao Ping head into a top-level meeting during a visit to Beijing, China, in December of 1975. Ambassador George Bush is behind the President.
(Gerald R. Ford Library.)

Leery about the possibility that Bush might suddenly emerge as a vice-presidential running mate with Ford, the Democrats demanded a promise that Bush would not be placed on the Republican ticket. It was an example of blatant partisanship, and Ford's instinct was to fight the conditional agreement. But because Bush was not so inclined, his nomination was approved.

That mild skirmish was just a taste of what lay ahead in the election year of 1976. Inside his own political party and out, Gerald Ford would be in for the fight of his life.

Chapter 11

The Battle for Ballots

When President Ford first learned of Ronald Reagan's plans to seek the Republican nomination for President in the political primaries, Ford dismissed the idea, considering Reagan still a relative lightweight of minor concern. As the new year opened, however, Ford realized there was nothing lightweight about Reagan's intentions. In a telephone conversation some weeks before, the challenger had told Ford that he hoped the primary battle would not be divisive or harmful to the Republican Party.

Ford could not see how it would not be. "I'm sorry you're getting into this," the President told Reagan. "I believe I've done a good job and that I can be elected. Regardless of your good intentions, your bid is bound to be divisive. It will take a lot of money, a lot of effort, and it will leave a lot of scars. It won't be helpful, no matter which of us wins the nomination." Reagan would not be dissuaded.

AN UPHILL STRUGGLE

On January 8, 1976, a Gallup poll was released that did little to brighten the spirits of President Ford and his staff. Of those people queried, 46 percent disapproved of Ford's presidential performance, 39 percent approved, and 15 percent could not make up their minds. Analyzing the possible reasoning behind the negative showing, staff members attributed some of it to lingering dissatisfaction with the Nixon pardon. Others felt the amnesty program for the Vietnam draft dodgers played a part. Still others complained that the President was being "run" by Secretary of State Henry Kissinger, whom many Americans distrusted. Then there were the squabbles with Congress over legislation. During his 2½ years in office, Ford vetoed 66 bills sent to him, 48 by regular veto and 18 by pocket veto (refusing to sign a bill within a designated period of time), and Congress overrode his veto 12 times.

Ford was also viewed as a career politician, one of the "good old boys" who understood the shadier aspects of wheeling and dealing in political backrooms. Individually, he was viewed as honest, likable, and sincere, but his associations hurt his image. Whatever the case, the incumbent knew he had an uphill struggle in order to win the nomination of his own party, and then take on the Democratic challenger.

Reagan's Strategy

Ford's past services and loyalty to the Republican Party won him the support and endorsement of party chieftains across the country. But Reagan's strategy was to organize the "troops," the many young newcomers to the political arena who were suspicious of those who had enjoyed power on the national level and who wanted to sweep clean with a new broom.

Also actively solicited by Reagan were those Republicans who were far more conservative than Ford. Some of these people viewed Ford's negotiations with the Soviet Union and China as becoming less defensive in our attitude toward these countries. And there were multitudes of Americans who viewed all Communists with contempt and wanted the United States to refrain from any relationships whatsoever.

Reagan made the most of those apprehensions, emphasizing that it was time for a new face with new ideas. Not only was his a new political face, it was a handsome one with instant recognition from roles in movies and on television. He knew how to work people's emotions, combining voice, facial features, and body gestures for maximum impact. Although Ford spoke clearly and effectively, his actions and appearance were those of a grown-up Boy Scout in the White House. It would, indeed, be a tough primary battle.

State of the Union Address

In his State of the Union address delivered on January 19, 1976, to both Houses of Congress, President Ford called for " a new realism that is true to the great principles upon which this nation was founded. We must introduce a new balance to our economy—a balance that favors not only sound, active government but also a much more vigorous, healthy economy that can create new jobs and hold down prices. We must introduce," Ford continued, "a new balance in the relationship between the individual and the government—a balance that favors greater individual freedom and self-reliance."

On the domestic front, Ford called for additional cuts in taxes and warned that government could not create jobs for everyone wanting to work. Private industry needed incentives and government regulations needed to be simplified. On the international level, Ford criticized legislation that had limited his powers in dealing with challenges beyond U.S. boundaries. Reform was needed in the realm of national intelligence, and cooperation was demanded to strengthen this area. "It is time to go beyond sensationalism," observed the President, "and ensure an effective, responsible and responsive intelligence capability."

Building an Image

After his address, Ford met personally with reporters to talk about his reduction in federal spending. It was an unusual strategy; in most cases, budget officials spell out the specifics of a President's overall program. But Ford wanted to show the public and the media that he indeed understood the intricacies of being the nation's chief executive. He was tired of opinion surveys that he was a "nice guy" who was in over his head in trying to handle the presidency.

While Ford handled matters on the home front, ever mindful of the first Republican primary on February 24 in New Hampshire, Henry Kissinger went to Moscow. Time was running out for progress on strategic arms reduction, and Ford desperately hoped for a breakthrough. Kissinger and Congress had never enjoyed a harmonious relationship, and Reagan was constantly accusing the secretary of state of having James Schlesinger fired. It would help the Ford re-election campaign considerably if Kissinger could somehow dent the Soviet position regarding arms.

PRIMARY VICTORIES

Manning the Oval Office restricted Ford's efforts to travel and campaign, while Ronald Reagan seemed to be everywhere in the country. But in a sense, the situation helped the President. If he had hopscotched the nation giving speeches, he might have been accused of being just another politician, a tag that was now being applied to Reagan. Instead, Ford appeared to be doing his job, with only an occasional political talk here and there. And his own political organization, which had been quite muddled in the beginning, became better organized. In the New Hampshire primary, Ford slipped by challenger Reagan with some 1,317 votes, 17 delegates to 4. It felt good to win an election outside of the Fifth Congressional District in Michigan, and Gerald Ford looked forward to the next primary contests. Subsequent victories in Massachusetts, Vermont, and Florida bolstered his hopes even further.

Was Reagan considering pulling out of the race? Not at all. He intensified his campaign, implying that American negotiations with the Soviet Union were rather lightweight ("a foreign policy whose principal accomplishment seems to be our acquisition of the right to sell Pepsi-Cola in Siberia . . ."). He also suggested that the United States was being too easy on the leftist leader of Panama ("I don't understand how the State Department can suggest we pay blackmail to this dictator, for blackmail is what it is."). Usually, in Reagan's critical speeches, he put Kissinger's name before Ford's, a carefully placed emphasis.

The Battle Intensifies

Reagan finally scored a primary victory in North Carolina, but a win in Illinois kept Ford substantially ahead. Then, rather than challenge Ford in the New York and Wisconsin primaries, Reagan pulled a surprise move. Recognizing Ford's strength in both states, the challenger went on national television and repeated his charges that the United States, "the last island of freedom," should not be consigned to "the dustbin of history."

Ford picked up the tempo of his own speaking style, adding a touch of humor. "Governor Reagan and I do have one thing in common. We both played football. I played for Michigan. He played for Warner Brothers." Ford swept through both Wisconsin and New York, but Reagan ran up wins in Texas,

Alabama, Georgia, and Indiana. Throughout the spring, the primary battle seesawed.

THE DEMOCRATIC TICKET

Meanwhile, a national unknown in the Democratic Party was picking up public support and delegate strength. Former Governor Jimmy Carter of Georgia seemed to emerge out of nowhere to capture the hearts (and Democratic primary votes) of Americans everywhere. But despite Carter's impressive showing in the Democratic primaries, Ford remained convinced that the presidential candidate the Democrats would select would be Hubert Humphrey of Minnesota, a former U.S. senator and Vice-President under Lyndon Johnson from 1965 to 1969. Humphrey was staying out of the primary skirmishes, letting the lesser-known Democrats fight it out amongst themselves.

But Ford's analysis of the Democratic situation proved incorrect. Throughout the spring, Carter continued to gain strength. Then, when the Democrats gathered in July at Madison Square Garden in New York City for their national convention, they selected Carter for the top slot on their ticket. They also chose Senator Walter Mondale of Minnesota (Humphrey's protegé) to be their vice-presidential candidate.

A Nervous Incumbent

During the Republican and Democratic primaries, there was a growing feeling against the longtime "politicos," a feeling that made the incumbent President nervous. Unlike Ford, Ronald Reagan was not associated with the Washington establishment, the Watergate affair, or Richard Nixon. Reagan was, in a sense, "Mr. Clean," and as the spring primaries intensified, his speeches became tougher.

Because both the international and domestic scenes remained relatively calm during this period, Ford was able to devote a little extra time to campaigning. On May 28, the United States and the Soviet Union signed a treaty limiting the size of underground nuclear explosions and permitting on-site inspections of testing facilities. Perhaps it was not a major step in arms reduction, but any step forward on the road to peace was worth notice.

Not only was 1976 a presidential election year, it was also the nation's bicentennial (200th) birthday. From January through December, big and small observances were held across the country. Ford used the opportunity to lead countless parades and give numerous speeches.

THE REPUBLICAN TICKET

In August, the Republicans held their national convention at the Kemper Sports Arena in Kansas City, Missouri. Going into the convention, Ford and Reagan stood neck and neck for their party's presidential nomination. Ford could claim 1,102 delegates, Reagan had 1,063, and 94 were uncommitted. Ford was 28 votes short for the nomination.

A political convention can be the best and the worst example of America's political process. Staff members of leading candidates will beg, promise, and basically "wheel and deal" for delegates, sometimes in open group and state gatherings, other times in backrooms and hallways. From August 16 to 19, that is exactly what happened in Kansas City. When the smoke finally cleared, Gerald Ford posted a slim victory of 1,187 votes on the first polling of delegates against 1,070 votes for Ronald Reagan. As his vice-presidential running mate, Ford selected Senator Robert Dole of Kansas.

THE ELECTION OF 1976

Having managed a narrow win over Reagan to capture the Republican presidential nomination, Ford now faced a battle to hold on to the White House. Jimmy Carter's strength lay in his lack of association and identification with the Washington establishment. Many people in the country harbored a suspicion about politicians at the national level. Bitterness still lingered about the Nixon pardon, and Reagan's determined drive to win the Republican nomination had divided the party. Ford had his work cut out for him.

Presidential Debates

By 1976 presidential debates had become a standard forum preceding a national election, and plans were made for Ford and Carter to face each other three times before election day on November 2. The televised events were scheduled for Philadelphia on September 23, San Francisco on October 6, and Williamsburg, Virginia, on October 22. Ford felt confident. He had beaten many congressional challengers before, and he would beat this opponent too. To prepare for the encounters, estimated to attract between 80 to 100 million viewers, Ford reviewed his own positions and studied re-runs of the Nixon-Kennedy debates.

Few surprises came out of the debates and the intermingling of campaign speeches. In the San Francisco debate, however, Ford made a statement that the Yugoslavians, Romanians, and Poles did not consider themselves dominated by the Soviet Union. This was immediately challenged by Carter and was considered a sizable "goof" on Ford's part by many watching. Questions were also raised about some of Ford's past political contributions, from whom and why, which did not help his image. In the final weeks of the campaign, Carter continued to draw strength from his position of being outside Watergate and Washington. He could lead an offensive charge, hurling criticisms, while Ford had to spend much of his time defending his own administration and past Republican wrong-doings.

Losing the Presidency

By the time voters went to the polls on November 2, the candidates were exhausted. In Grand Rapids, Jerry and Betty Ford voted early. Just before boarding a plane to return to Washington, a mural was dedicated at the Kent County airport depicting the President as an Eagle Scout, as a high school football player, as the driver of a Model-T Ford, and as a smiling bridegroom. There was also a newspaper headline from 1974: FORD BECOMES PRESIDENT. It was a moving moment as Ford fought hard for self-control. Hopefully, that headline would be repeated.

But it was not to be. Jimmy Carter was elected President with 40,830,763 popular votes (55.20 percent) and 297 electoral votes. Gerald Ford posted 39,147,793 popular votes (44.61 percent) and 240 electoral votes. It hurt to lose, but Ford found comfort in a thought expressed by his son Jack. "When you come so close, it's really hard to lose," said the young man, who had campaigned for his father. "But at the same time, if you can't lose as graciously as you planned to win, then you shouldn't have been in the thing in the first place."

They were kind words, wise and gentle. Jerry Ford could not have said it better himself.

Chapter 12

A Different Niche

January 20, 1977, dawned clear and cold in Washington, D.C. At precisely 12:05 P.M. on a platform erected on the east portico of the Capitol, Jimmy Carter of Georgia took the oath as the 39th President of the United States. The event included all the gala trappings of a presidential inauguration—the bands, the parade, the crowds, and the applause—everything that Gerald Ford had missed in assuming both the vice-presidency and the presidency.

But there was no looking back. Once the new President had taken the oath of office, his first words were, "For myself and for our nation I want to thank my predecessor for all he has done to heal our land." The expression was clearly genuine, an unexpected gesture. As the audience applauded, Gerald Ford acknowledged their cheers by rising, then he leaned over and shook Carter's hand.

NEW ROLES

After the official ceremonies were over, there were the final good-byes to the Rockefellers, the Kissingers, the Cabinet members, the White House staff—all trusted and true workers and friends. Signs waved "Good Luck" and "Thank you, Jerry," and a band played "God Bless America." After handshakes, tears, and hugs, the former President and his weary entourage boarded a plane to return to Grand Rapids. After 28 years of public service, Gerald Ford was now just a man out of a job.

Not for long, however. Soon Ford began receiving offers to serve on the boards of many leading American companies where he could continue to lend his counsel and leadership. Universities and colleges sought him as a public speaker. Although removed from the day-to-day activities in the nation's capital, Ford's help was requested by President Carter, and later, by President Ronald Reagan, in lining up congressional votes for such matters as the Panama Canal treaty, the recognition of China, the sale of weapons to Saudi Arabia, and efforts to curb presidential powers.

Operating from his retirement home and office in Palm Springs, California, Ford enjoyed the luxury of playing golf all year long. He especially appreciated the opportunity of playing the game as part of charity affairs to raise money for worthy causes. "Now the guy can swing a club without worrying about a hundred photographers catching him slice the ball," quipped comedian Bob Hope, a favorite partner. For his own part, Ford enjoyed the different niche he had found.

"An Extraordinary Individual"

In 1979 Ford wrote and published his autobiography, *A Time to Heal*. It revealed a behind-the-scene look at recent events through the eyes and mind of a man who had lived through some of the most turbulent times in American history. "A normal person would have lost his sanity," observed one reviewer, "but Gerald Ford was, fortunately, an extraordinary individual." On April 27, 1981, he dedicated the Gerald R. Ford Library in Ann Arbor, on the campus of the University of Michigan.

In 1981 President Ronald Reagan asked former Presidents Nixon, Ford, and Carter to represent the United States at the funeral of Anwar Sadat, the Egyptian leader who was assassinated during a military parade. There was a tenseness in the airplane carrying the distinguished passengers to Egypt, but by the time they returned, Ford and Carter had become friends and were calling each other "Jerry" and "Jimmy." Soon they were planning to serve as hosts for public policy forums; they have also assisted in "get-out-the vote" efforts during presidential elections.

IN RETROSPECT

The perspective of time will provide historians a better yardstick to objectively evaluate the presidency of Gerald Ford. Few would deny that he inherited a government severely tainted by corrupt practices and misdeeds, yet he managed to heal many of the wounds that had been inflicted. As the former President once observed:

> It is easy to make judgments after the fact, but I can honestly say that while events were happening, I was guided by a God in whom I have always had faith, my wife and family, and the good of the nation. I gave it my best shot and I offer no apologies. The people in this nation have been good to me, and I would like to think I have given them something of value in return.

Restoring Spirit and Trust

Even Ford's strongest critics have awarded the man from Grand Rapids high marks in the areas of integrity, tact, and perseverance. As House Minority Leader, he won the respect of both Republicans and Democrats in spite of the virtually impossible task during the Nixon years of having to work with a White House that sought little congressional cooperation and consultation. Upon moving into the executive office himself, Ford found himself plagued by an inflationary economy as well as major social and political divisions. Dedicated and determined, he structured a variety of programs to revive the nation's financial strength, maintain open communications with other countries, and restore the positive spirit of Americans at home and abroad.

Ford's efforts revealed no brilliant economic strategies or dynamic innovations in foreign policy, but rather a cautious, careful methodology. Early evaluations of his 2½ years as President suggest that he succeeded in restoring some trust in the American political system while causing no daring or dangerous shifts in the country's domestic and foreign policies.

Bibliography

Beard, Charles A. *The Presidents in American History.* New York: Julian Messner, 1985. This compilation of data about the Presidents, Washington through Reagan, offers but a brief entry about Gerald Ford. Nonetheless, the information is factual and objective.

Ford, Gerald R. *A Time to Heal.* New York: Harper & Row, 1979. There is hardly a better source about a man and his presidency than the subject himself. In this memoir, Ford provides a look at his past, present, and thoughts on the future. His feelings about Watergate and the Nixon pardon are particularly intriguing.

Kane, Joseph Nathan. *Facts About the Presidents.* New York: H.W. Wilson, 1981. A vital reference tool crammed full of useful facts, Kane's book is one of the most compact and fascinating collections of data about the Presidents available.

Mercer, Charles. *Gerald Ford.* New York: G. P. Putnam's Sons, 1975. Aimed primarily at younger readers, this easy-to-read biography offers a quick look at the nation's 38th chief executive. The anecdotes are well chosen.

Sipiera, Paul P. *Gerald Ford.* Chicago: Childrens Press, 1989. The facts are accurate, the style is fluid, and the volume is especially intended for the reader who appreciates many pictures with the text. The chronology at the back of the book is a worthwhile touch.

Sullivan, George. *Mr. President.* New York: Dodd Mead, 1984. The author offers a capsule look at all the chief executives through President Reagan. The articles at the beginning of the volume, which include write-ups on such political potpourri as primaries, conventions, and the electoral college, add to the book's usefulness.

terHorst, Jerald F. *Gerald Ford and the Future of the Presidency.* New York: The Third Press, 1974. A former White House Press secretary, terHorst was in a unique position to write this volume. Actually, the book is both a biography of Gerald Ford and an analysis of the Watergate affair and its effect on the presidency.

White, Theodore H. *The Making of the President 1972.* New York: Antheneum Publishers, 1973. Anyone wishing to understand the American political system and the electoral process should read one of White's accounts of a presidential election. The 1972 chronicle is particularly valuable in examining not only the "roadmap" followed by the ultimate winner, Richard Nixon, but in noting the actions taken by such Republican Party powers as Gerald Ford.

Index

PRESIDENTS OF THE UNITED STATES

GEORGE WASHINGTON	L. Falkof	0-944483-19-4
JOHN ADAMS	R. Stefoff	0-944483-10-0
THOMAS JEFFERSON	R. Stefoff	0-944483-07-0
JAMES MADISON	B. Polikoff	0-944483-22-4
JAMES MONROE	R. Stefoff	0-944483-11-9
JOHN QUINCY ADAMS	M. Greenblatt	0-944483-21-6
ANDREW JACKSON	R. Stefoff	0-944483-08-9
MARTIN VAN BUREN	R. Ellis	0-944483-12-7
WILLIAM HENRY HARRISON	R. Stefoff	0-944483-54-2
JOHN TYLER	L. Falkof	0-944483-60-7
JAMES K. POLK	M. Greenblatt	0-944483-04-6
ZACHARY TAYLOR	D. Collins	0-944483-17-8
MILLARD FILLMORE	K. Law	0-944483-61-5
FRANKLIN PIERCE	F. Brown	0-944483-25-9
JAMES BUCHANAN	D. Collins	0-944483-62-3
ABRAHAM LINCOLN	R. Stefoff	0-944483-14-3
ANDREW JOHNSON	R. Stevens	0-944483-16-X
ULYSSES S. GRANT	L. Falkof	0-944483-02-X
RUTHERFORD B. HAYES	N. Robbins	0-944483-23-2
JAMES A. GARFIELD	F. Brown	0-944483-63-1
CHESTER A. ARTHUR	R. Stevens	0-944483-05-4
GROVER CLEVELAND	D. Collins	0-944483-01-1
BENJAMIN HARRISON	R. Stevens	0-944483-15-1
WILLIAM McKINLEY	D. Collins	0-944483-55-0
THEODORE ROOSEVELT	R. Stefoff	0-944483-09-7
WILLIAM H. TAFT	L. Falkof	0-944483-56-9
WOODROW WILSON	D. Collins	0-944483-18-6
WARREN G. HARDING	A. Canadeo	0-944483-64-X
CALVIN COOLIDGE	R. Stevens	0-944483-57-7

HERBERT C. HOOVER	B. Polikoff	0-944483-58-5
FRANKLIN D. ROOSEVELT	M. Greenblatt	0-944483-06-2
HARRY S. TRUMAN	D. Collins	0-944483-00-3
DWIGHT D. EISENHOWER	R. Ellis	0-944483-13-5
JOHN F. KENNEDY	L. Falkof	0-944483-03-8
LYNDON B. JOHNSON	L. Falkof	0-944483-20-8
RICHARD M. NIXON	R. Stefoff	0-944483-59-3
GERALD R. FORD	D. Collins	0-944483-65-8
JAMES E. CARTER	D. Richman	0-944483-24-0
RONALD W. REAGAN	N. Robbins	0-944483-66-6
GEORGE H.W. BUSH	R. Stefoff	1-56074-033-7

GARRETT EDUCATIONAL CORPORATION
130 EAST 13TH STREET
ADA, OK 74820